MAHALIA JACKSON
QUEEN OF GOSPEL SONG

MAHALIA JACKSON
QUEEN OF GOSPEL SONG

BY
LESLIE GOURSE

An Impact Biography
Franklin Watts
A Division of Grolier Publishing
New York London Hong Kong Sydney
Danbury, Connecticut

Photographs copyright ©: Brown Brothers: pp.129, 135 bottom; The Bettman
Archive: pp. 130, 131, 132 inset, 136; UPI/Bettman: pp. 130 inset, 134 top,
136 top, 136 bottom left, 137, 140 top, 143, 144; Archive photos/Frank Driggs
Collection: p. 131 inset; Archive photos: p. 140 bottom; Retna Ltd.: p. 132 (David
Redfern); Frank Driggs Collection: p. 133; AP/Wide World Photos: pp. 134 bottom,
135 top, 138, 139 (both photos), 141, 142 (both photos).

Library of Congress Cataloging-in-Publication Data

Mahalia Jackson: queen of gospel song / by Leslie Gourse.
p. cm. — (An Impact biography)
Includes bibliographical references (p. 119) and index.
Summary: Traces the rise of the famous gospel singer from her early youth
in New Orleans to her Chicago-based musical career.
ISBN 0-531-11228-4
1. Jackson, Mahalia, 1911–1972—Juvenile literature. 2. Gospel
musicians—United States—Biography—Juvenile literature. [1. Jackson, Mahalia,
1911–1972. 2. Singers. 3. Women—Biography. 4. Afro-Americans—Biography.]
I. Title.
ML3930.J2G86   1996
782.25'4'092—dc20   95-49845
[B]   CIP   MN

CONTENTS

FOR
WILGIE FULTON MCLEOD

Mahalia Jackson

Queen of Gospel Song

THE LEGEND OF
MAHALIA JACKSON

Mahalia Jackson, who was born into a very poor family on October 26, 1911, in New Orleans, found her greatest joy was singing gospel music in her family's little Baptist church. The music gave her the strength and courage to face her daily trials. Her mother died when she was only five years old, and she lived with a very strict aunt, who made her work hard and even forced her to leave school before she was a teenager. Mahalia devoted herself so completely to singing gospel, and she was so gifted, that she would grow up to be the greatest gospel singer the world has ever known. She became a symbol and a source of strength and spirituality for African-Americans, and not only for religious, churchgoing people but for all people, including whites, who felt committed to the civil rights struggle in the country. She was also an uplifting figure for anyone with any kind of trouble. Mahalia's voice and religious fervor had a healing quality.

Even as a little child, she had such a powerful and beautiful voice that everyone loved to listen to her. Determined to escape the poverty and total segregation of her hometown neighborhood, which was nicknamed Pinching Town, she went to live in Chicago when she was a teenager. Right away she started singing in a Baptist church, and then she traveled around the country, singing in many churches. For more than twenty years, she sang primarily for African-American Baptists. She sang for them in great and small churches, some of them just humble storefronts, and at their conventions.

Until she was in her late thirties, she earned very little money. At that time, she began recording for the little Apollo label that distributed her records around the country. Word of her genius began to spread outside the church world. In 1950, she was invited to sing in Carnegie Hall. After that, she became the most important star representing the gospel world, and she traveled to sing for kings and queens, presidents and prime ministers. Mahalia also kept going back to sing in churches for the people who had loved her singing first and had launched her in her career as the queen of gospel music.

She never sang the blues, or jazz, or popular music of any kind. Despite poverty and hardships for so many years, she insisted on singing only the gospel. That was her greatest joy in life. She called herself "a hardshell Baptist," meaning that she was a very devout, strict, Southern Baptist, who believed with all her heart in the Bible. Her singing was so inspiring and exciting that her audiences cheered, cried, and called out to her: "Amen," and "Yes, Lord." She used her creamy contralto voice to sing "The Lord's Prayer," and she could hit beautiful soprano notes that made people cry. She could holler, too, for rousing spirituals. People not only shouted encouragement; they swayed and danced with her. Sometimes they even fainted in churches when they heard her exultant praises of the Lord.

At first, in some of the more conservative churches, Mahalia's style was considered too spirited, too swinging, and too jazzy. She shook her body, clapped her hands, and sometimes got down on her knees or danced around on the stage and skipped in the aisles. That was normal for gospel singers, especially those under the influence of the Sanctified or Pentecostal or Revivalist churches, but not for the strict Baptist churches. Mahalia and many other gospel singers in the Baptist churches favored the Sanctified style of singing and praying. When she sang the hymn "Move on up a Little Higher," she pulled her skirt up an inch, then another inch. But when she was criticized by a minister in church for her exuberance, she stood up for herself in front of the congregation by quoting the scriptures: "Make a joyful noise unto the Lord, as David said," she explained.

"All I do is add a little bounce," she often said about her down-home, southern style, which she had developed in New Orleans. "The bounce in my music simply means stepping up the tempo and putting joy in the voice." And, "I put everything I am into it." One friend explained, "Mahalia doesn't believe that God exists. She knows he does."

Many times people advised her to become a blues singer, because she could earn more money in the entertainment world. But Mahalia never wanted to use her singing to sell whiskey in a nightclub, she said. She thought that putting gospel songs to that use was "a mess."

After she kept her promise to the Lord to sing only gospel for about thirty years, her big voice and enormous talent burst out of the confines of her church-centered world. White audiences began to hear her performances in concerts and to appreciate the gospel, a type of singing that had not really become very popular even among African-Americans until the 1930s. At that time, the Depression, when the banks failed in America, sent people running to churches for spiritual courage. Her audiences grew. When Mahalia was thirty-eight in 1950, she became the first gospel singer to perform at Carnegie Hall. Europeans heard her recordings, honored her, and invited her to travel and sing in person for them. For the last third of her life, she was an international star. She stunned white and Asian people, who thought her voice seemed to come from beyond. The Prime Minister of India, Mrs. Indira Gandhi, once missed top-level government meetings to stay at one of Mahalia's concerts. Mahalia sang for ninety minutes beyond the appointed time of the concert.

She was totally untutored in classical music; she created her own style. She did it by listening to her elders who preached and sang in church. Their spirit and techniques for expressing themselves as religious people bound together in a community, with all their special hardships as African-Americans, taught her important early lessons. She drank in the cadences of the preacher's voice, then responded with the hums and moans and shouts of the congregation. The spirit with which a person sang was more important than the song or a singer's voice quality. In the church, and only in the church in those days, African-Americans could relax and be themselves. Mahalia found joy in that freedom and communion with others. And her spirit as well as her beautiful voice made her a natural leader among people singing the gospel. She had absolutely no need for classical singing techniques. They would have actually gotten in her way.

She sang with naturalness, directly to people. Her breaths occasionally came in the middle of words, and her idiosyncratic, New Orleans accent produced "oith" for the word "earth." She used every iota of her New Orleans background, with its heritage of merry, spirited music, to her best advantage for her purposes. Her heavenly vibrato and rapturous embellishments helped create the glorious sound of her total conviction. One of her favorite songs was the old spiritual "Didn't It Rain!" No more exciting version of this song exists than Mahalia's on a recording she made at the Newport Jazz Festival in Newport, Rhode Island, in 1958. "Talk about rain all night, Oh, my Lord, Oh, didn't it rain, rain forty days, forty nights, without stopping . . . Knock on the window, knock on the door, Brother Noah, can't you take on more . . . full of sin . . . God got the key, can't get in." Her audience roared. Some people at the concert that rainy night claimed that, once she sang that song, the rain stopped.

She could sing any religious song, and no matter how simple or unimportant it was, she made it transcendent. She could give the deceptively simple "I'm on My Way (to Canaan Land)," with its repeated lyrics, her full, swinging, bouncy, percussive, soulful treatment. Nobody could clap with more authority than Mahalia. Sometimes people in her audiences tried to clap the way she did, but most people who did

14

not come out of a gospel-singing background couldn't imitate her great sense of rhythm.

When an engineer in a recording studio tried to tell her how to sing a gospel song, she asked him how he could have the nerve to tell her how to sing. "That song was born in my mouth," she said. Her authority over her music was total, and she communicated a sense of holy purpose and spiritual joy to many of the great civil rights events of the century. Singing at the Lincoln Memorial for the civil rights March on Washington in 1963, she herself became a kind of bridge—a precious link—between the races in a time of crisis.

As years went on, young people would ask her for help in achieving success. She would tell them that she was trying. And if God could take her out of the scrubbing pots—for she had worked as a washerwoman for many years—He could lift them up, too. They must simply be patient.

The truth is that patience played a small part in the story of Mahalia's rise to become a legend in the annals of folk and sacred music. Even more important was her musical genius and fiery spiritual commitment to gospel music and the uplifting of African-American people. Her voice, propelled by her personality, was a voice that came "once in a millennium," said the Reverend Martin Luther King Jr., the great civil rights leader and pastor of the Ebenezer Baptist Church in Atlanta, Georgia, where she sang when her fame began to grow.

When she died, one of the toughest mayors in American history, Mayor Richard Daley of Chicago, arranged for her to lie in state there for a day of official mourning. Mahalia had spent her adult life with Chicago as home base and become friends with many politicians. She had even paved the way for Reverend King to lead a civil rights demonstration in Chicago. Mayor Daley would not have welcomed him if it hadn't been for Mahalia's influence.

Far more than an entertainer, she had put her gift to use to serve people. From Chicago, she was taken back to her native New Orleans for a traditional funeral with a marching band. Few women ever had that honor. But she had been one of the tiny number of singers who could move audiences of all

15

backgrounds mysteriously and suddenly to tears of joy and sorrow. For African-Americans, who were gospel fans and had loved Mahalia's singing for most of her life, her voice was a force that had come from within the spirit. The rest of the world came to agree.

2

A NEW ORLEANS
GIRLHOOD

Mahalia's memories of her childhood in New Orleans would always be bittersweet. She had to leave school and work full-time after she finished the eighth grade. And she was always profoundly saddened by the poverty and prejudice against African-Americans. But she found joy and fun in the small Baptist church where she attended services and joined in community activities with other children nearly every day. She loved the musical style of the preacher's sermons. Above all, she adored singing gospel hymns in the congregation of the little Mount Moriah Baptist Church.

"All around me I could hear the feet tapping and the hands clapping. That gave me bounce. I liked it much better than being up in the choir singing. I liked to sing the songs the folks sing which testify to the glory of the Lord—those anthems are too dead and cold," she would tell *Time* magazine for an article published on October 4, 1954. The driving songs deepened her belief in the Lord. Her devotion took her mind off her everyday cares and filled her with the only hope and contentment she knew as a child.

Mahalia's great-grandmother and great-grandfather on her mother's side had been slaves on a rice plantation in Legonier, in the countryside far from New Orleans. Mahalia called that area "the deep country." Her father's parents had been born there, too. After the Civil War, when they were set free, the families remained on the land as sharecroppers, raising crops on land they leased from the former plantation owner. Mahalia's family was always in debt for the goods they had to buy from the landowners. An African-American could spend ten years trying to pay off the price of a mule, for example, and find out that the mule still didn't belong to him. The problem often lay in the calculations by the landowners.

Mahalia always referred to her people as "Negro" and "colored" in those days. African-American children went to school only when it rained. Otherwise they were supposed to work in the fields. Most of the social life for Mahalia's family and their friends revolved around their Baptist church. They were devout believers in God; all of them were baptized in the water of the nearby Chafalaye River, which fed into the Mississippi. As children and adolescents, Mahalia's aunts and uncles and friends prepared themselves for the joy of their baptism. The oldest, most respected people in church prayed for them, and then, when the young people were considered morally ready, they were taken to the river and submerged there. They came up shouting for joy, thrilled to be accepted spiritually and totally by the Lord and their community. Their baptism and faith were among the greatest rewards they would ever have in their impoverished lives.

One of Mahalia's uncles, who was named Porter, was disgusted at the lack of earthly opportunities for his family. Instead of working in the fields, he began helping out the U.S. Army Corps of Engineers, whose riverboats were carrying on a special project on the Chafalaye River.

Eventually a white steamboat captain befriended Porter and took him onto his boat. Uncle Porter learned to become a cook on the coal and wood stoves there, then on other little steamboats. He worked on a great variety of boats on southern rivers, including the mail boats that ran between

Natchez, Mississippi, and New Orleans, Louisiana. He started taking his brothers and sisters from Legonier to New Orleans, the big city. There the women found jobs as laundresses, maids, and cooks for the white people in town.

Mahalia's mother, Charity Clark, Porter's sister, fell in love with a man she had grown up with in Legonier; his name was Johnny Jackson, and he, too, had migrated to New Orleans. He worked as a longshoreman, moving cotton on the river docks when he could get a day's work, cutting people's hair in a barbershop some nights, and preaching without pay in a Baptist church on Sundays. Even with all those part-time jobs, he didn't earn much money and didn't have a penny to spare. He and Charity had one child, Mahalia, born on October 26, 1911.

Charity already had a son, Peter Roosevelt Hunter, born in Legonier in 1906. Before she and Johnny Jackson had gotten together in New Orleans, Johnny had lived with another woman and had two sons with her. He and Charity never lived together under the same roof. They were too poor to get their own house.

So Charity lived in one house with some of her six sisters who had come from Legonier. Mahalia's father lived with his parents in another house. Eventually he went to live with another woman, whom he married. In those days, African-Americans called themselves married in Louisiana, even if they hadn't gone through a legal ceremony under what they called white law. They had good, practical reasons. The law strongly favored the rights of husbands over their wives. Women feared that they could become financially responsible for men and that men could take advantage of them in many ways. Under the conditions and customs that prevailed, Mahalia's parents never got married under white law, but she was registered at birth as a Jackson.

Mahalia's parents were very religious, churchgoing people. Mahalia could not remember a time when she wasn't going to church nearly every day and singing there. She had a big voice even when she was three years old, and so she attracted attention and admiration. Two of her cousins on her father's side were entertainers with an act in show business.

They toured the South, and they wanted to take Mahalia with them, because of her lovely singing voice. Mahalia's mother refused to let the child go. "And she didn't have a dime when she said no to them," Mahalia would later recall. "It's easy to be independent when you've got money. But to be independent when you haven't got a thing—that's the Lord's test."

Mahalia's life was carefree; nicknamed Little Halie, she felt that she was the pet of the family, until she was five years old. That year, her mother became ill. Mahalia didn't realize what was happening. She knew that she was allowed to run a little wild, going in and out of the house whenever she pleased, while her mother stayed in bed and her aunts went to work. The family's routine was upset. Then her mother died.

Mahalia never knew exactly what her mother's trouble had been. "They took her back to the country town where our family had come from. I remember a wagon met the train and carried us to the river," Mahalia said for her own book, *Movin' on Up*, written with Evan McLeod Wylie. "They put the casket in a little white skiff and we got in another. . . . The memory of that little white skiff [being rowed to a cemetery] still lives in my mind, but I was too young then to understand sorrow."

It's possible that Charity died from an illness related to undernourishment. Mahalia had been born with an eye infection, and her eyes had to be washed constantly. Her aunts kept her in the dark until she was able to open her eyes and see well. Furthermore, she was born with very bowed legs, probably from rickets resulting from nutritional deficiencies. It took her many years of eating very well—such things as vegetables from the family garden and shrimps and crayfish from the waters around New Orleans—for her to cure herself and make her legs straight.

Soon after Mahalia was born, her mother returned to her job. Mahalia was nursed by an aunt who had just had a child of her own. Mahalia was used to being looked after by her aunts. After her mother died, they had a discussion about who would raise her and her brother, Peter, then ten years old. One of the aunts, Mahala Paul, for whom Mahalia had been named, decided that she would take both children into her shack. (Actually, Mahalia was named Mahala, too, but she would change her own name to make it special, ornamenting it with an "i," as she was growing up.)

Mahala Paul was nicknamed Duke, probably because she looked people straight in the eye and communicated a sense of power and authority. She was a very stern, bossy woman. Even in her strict, churchgoing family, Aunt Duke was considered a hard, sometimes cruel, taskmaster. A large woman with a very straight back, she worked hard as a cook for a white family in one of the best sections of New Orleans. Because she was such a good cook, she earned ten dollars a week— "high pay for a colored woman in those days," Mahalia would later say proudly. The family's rent for the shack was six to eight dollars a month, so there was nothing left over for toys or frills. Like many poor children at that time in New Orleans, Mahalia went without necessities.

"I was allowed one dress and went barefoot all the time," she recalled for *Movin' on Up.* "When it came time to get dressed up on Saturday or Sunday, we children used to bathe our legs and rub them with Vaseline to make them shine. We took our baths in the kitchen and heated the hot water in the stove or out in the yard in the sun in one of those big number three tin tubs."

They lived in a shack on Water Street at Audubon Street, in a community of poor black people, between the railroad tracks and the Mississippi River levee. Mahalia called their home "a little old shotgun shack." Whenever the sun shone outside, it shone through the holes in the roof, too, and when it rained outside, the water came right through the holes. The family was always setting out pots and pans to catch the water and sweeping the place with brooms. The shotgun shacks where the poor people lived were so named because someone could fire a shotgun at the front door and have the bullet go straight through the house and out the back window.

When she wasn't cooking, Aunt Duke devoted her life to the church, going to services and taking part in women's organizations—benevolent societies, Mahalia called them.

Because Aunt Duke made a meager living, the children in her house—her son Freddie, Mahalia, and Peter—had to help make ends meet. So, from her first days with Aunt Duke, Mahalia learned the meaning of hardship. If she didn't behave and work hard all the time, Duke punished the child with a cat-o'-nine-tails, a leather strap that parents in those days often used to hit their children.

Aunt Duke's husband, Emmanuel Paul, was an affectionate man who was kind to Mahalia. Her own father, however, having married another woman with whom he had children, tended to ignore her. She would reminisce that she often saw her father at the barbershop where he cut hair at night. "He put me on his lap and called me his chocolate drop," she said. He was never angry at her and never hit her. He gave her money to take home to Aunt Duke, she told some writers.

But a writer named Laurraine Goreau, who came to know Mahalia very well over a period of years, and wrote a book called *Just Mahalia, Baby*, said the truth was usually quite different. Mahalia's father didn't like her coming to the barbershop, because he didn't want his new family to see her. She tried to make up for the deformity of her very bowed legs by learning to run fast and play with as much strength as other children had. But she wasn't a pretty child. Several times her father made her get out of the shop, and he refused to give her money for shoes when Aunt Duke wouldn't buy any for her. He didn't become proud of her until she won fame as a gospel singer. Then he told everyone, "That's my daughter!"

She had plenty of chores to do around Aunt Duke's shack, because her brother, Peter, went to work as a yardboy for a white family. Mahalia scrubbed the floors with red brick and lye, until the cypress wood was bleached pale blond, she recalled in *Movin' on Up*. She also learned to make the family's mattresses from corn shucks and soft gray Spanish moss that hung from the trees. She gathered the moss and corn shucks in summertime and sewed them into mattress covers made from bleached cotton cement sacks. And she was also proud of having learned how to weave cane chairs from sugarcane stalks and palm fronds.

Another aunt, Bessie, who had been Charity's youngest sister, came to live with Aunt Duke's family, too. Bessie, who was twelve when Mahalia was five, already had a job. She used to take Mahalia with her to the house of a white family named Snyder to help get the children dressed for school. Then the girls washed the family's dishes and went to school, too. At the Snyders' house, Mahalia never felt a strong difference between herself and white people. The Snyders gave her excellent food and clothes, for which she was grateful, she said. "Growing up, I knew that some of the children I played with were white. I was colored, but it made no difference. In my day, Negro and white children rode together on the merry-go-round at Audubon Park. White and black lived next door to each other in our neighborhood and no issue was made of it. As a little girl, I used to play with a lot of Italian children, and when we had a spat, when those boys meddled with me, I hit them right back good and hard. But there were no hard feelings on their part and I didn't feel they were picking on me because I was colored." In the afternoon, after school, she and Bessie went back to the Snyders' house to do little odd jobs, for which they were paid two dollars a week.

Bessie soon had a child of her own. Mahalia was forced to drop out of school and stay home with Bessie's baby, while Bessie went to work. Mahalia was very upset at having to leave school. She had been very good at mathematics. And she often daydreamed about finding a way to a better life.

So she paid a great deal of attention to the neighborhood she grew up in, to try to educate herself about the world. Near her house was a ferryboat that took people across the river to another town, where some men had jobs. Men also worked on the banana boats along the busy waterfront, and in a coal yard, and on a train that traveled to and from a sugar refinery. The refinery was near the sugarcane and rice fields. A whiskey distillery and a gambling house were also nearby. Mahalia saw

African-Americans doing most of the heavy labor in these places. She knew their lives were especially hard, but she never talked about their troubles with bitterness, only with sympathy.

Among her favorite laborers were the men who worked as engineers on the train. They often put the children in the last car, which was called the caboose, or in the first car, and they traveled to the sugarcane refinery. There the men gave the children sugarcane to suck.

Aunt Duke used to take Mahalia to the meetings of all the benevolent societies, because Mahalia could read and write. She acted as a secretary and wrote down the notes of all the meetings. That chore kept Mahalia from socializing with her friends as much as she wanted to. She felt that she was more mature and serious than her friends, because she spent so much time with older people. The chores made her sad, but at the same time she met a few professional people—a doctor, a nurse, and several teachers. She thought she would like to grow up to be like them. She especially thought it would be great to be a nurse. But she had little hope for her own future in New Orleans.

She saw children carrying loads of laundry on their heads or on their backs from the white neighborhoods. Their mothers did the laundry for seventy-five cents a load. And she listened to peddlers hawking bananas and vegetables as they rolled through her neighborhood. They chanted, "We have bananas today" or "We have vegetables today." Mahalia thought their tone sounded very sad.

She was particularly unhappy during the week of Mardi Gras, because she noticed that African-Americans worked all year to earn money, spent it on their gowns and costumes, and put on their masks for the celebrations in the streets. Then some of them were killed. Mardi Gras was a time when members of clubs and societies, some with Indian names, chose to settle old arguments or debts, or simply tried to make members of other groups bow low to them. Murderers hid behind their masks. Nobody was ever charged with a crime. Mahalia thought the parade floats carrying the queen, which the white people sent down the main part of Canal Street, were beautiful. But the violent part of Mardi Gras made the celebration "a horrible sight," she would always feel. She was upset that her own people sometimes got into trouble of their own making.

Though her personal experience with whites as a little girl was pleasant, she grew up to become increasingly distressed because whites harassed African-Americans under the strict policy of segregation in New Orleans. The city had always been a busy port ruled at various times by the English, the Spanish, and the French. Then it became part of the United States under the Louisiana Purchase by America from France. There had always been a lot of mixing of different cultures and races in this sparkling Caribbean-type city. An entire class of people of mixed race—the Creoles—came into existence, and the white fathers of talented and bright Creole children of mixed race sent them to Europe to study. But by the early part of the twentieth century, segregation was enacted by law. Anyone with a background of mixed race—anyone who had even a tiny percentage of native African heritage—was classified as nonwhite, or Negro. And society was divided into Negro and white.

Mahalia noticed that some African-American youngsters hung around saloons and pool halls. She herself never went to those places, nor did the churchgoing people she lived among. But she knew that some people who went to them were decent people simply looking for a little recreation. And the police system could be very bad and hard on them. They might be arrested, jailed, beaten, and killed just for standing around in their own communities. If an African-American man resisted arrest, he could be killed. And if trouble really did break out between African-Americans, and the police came, the situation usually ended up with more trouble. A policeman might kill an African-American man and say the man had been trying to kill a policeman. Sometimes, Mahalia thought, an African-American might really have tried to fight back, because a man was a man.

"That made us feel we didn't have any protection. We didn't have any Negro lawyers that I ever knew of," she would recall. Unless an African-American man was well known and liked by whites, he could have a very hard time

25

with the police and the judges. So African-Americans would run when they saw police. If they were caught, their parents had to spend their last cent to get the kids out of jail. During Prohibition, when African-Americans made corn liquor or simply frequented speakeasies, the police conducted raids and arrested people. A lot of money changed hands so that African-American men could get out of jail. Then they went back to work making and selling liquor. Often it was the best way they had to support themselves or their families. "These people weren't bad people. But man has always been known to drink. But it was against the law to have these speakeasies in that time," Mahalia said, recalling the situation.

Preachers were the only African-Americans with influence. They went to the courts and asked judges to be lenient. Parents relied on ministers for help even if their children were convicted of serious crimes. Ministers conducted their lives in a way that everyone respected. So judges were merciful to people represented by ministers. "The minister was the only mouthpiece that the Negro had," Mahalia said.

She took refuge from her sadness in several ways. She often wandered around the riverfront, where she picked up driftwood she found floating in the river or washed up on the levee. She let the wood dry in the very hot sun and then took it home so the family would have wood to cook with and to heat the shack in winter. Sometimes she took an ax with her and cut up wood from old barges that were lying around. It wasn't strange in those days for a girl to be seen cutting wood for kindling. She loved to go to the riverfront, because she was able to get away from the drudgery of her home life. The sight of the mighty brown churning Mississippi River put a spell on her. There was something magical and exotic about the river. It was always busy with boat traffic for people of many races, nationalities, and cultures. "I felt a certain joy there," she would recall of her meditative periods by the river. She was always a child who thought about the future, she said. "I had this feeling that I could live better."

Music was her other great diversion. She learned quickly that New Orleans was a city where people believed in living for the moment and being as happy as they could. "It was a merry city," she said, having observed another of its good points. As poor and harassed as they were, people left their jobs on Friday and "started good timing," she recalled, "from Friday all the way through to Blue Monday. They wouldn't work on Monday. They'd just have this good time. A lot of people never did worry about getting rich. . . . Though people didn't have nothing, they simply did have a wonderful spirit under all that segregation there. The Negroes had their own enjoyment and tragedies, and somehow or other they went along."

People went to private clubs, lodges, cafés, and cabarets, where they played music and danced. There were still showboats on the Mississippi River. The musicians played a style of music that would become known as Dixieland, and eventually as jazz, but in those days, it was simply called music. It blended the musical styles of all the cultures that had passed through New Orleans, from the Africans to the French, the Indians, the Spanish, the English, and even the Caribbean people whose boats docked in New Orleans. In Mahalia's family, however, jazz wasn't acceptable. Even though it had a syncopated beat, which emphasized the weak beat in a measure of music and gave it real spark, just as the gospel songs in church did, jazz was played for common people in the honky-tonks and saloons.

But Mahalia knew very well what it was. She heard it in the streets played by such musicians as cornetist and band-leader King Oliver; his protégé, cornetist Louis Armstrong; Papa Celestin, another well-known local musician; and cornetist Bunk Johnson. Brass bands played jazz on trucks that went through the streets to entertain. On weekends they played at picnics and fish fries in the parks beside Lake Pontchartrain, the other great body of water bordering New Orleans. New Orleans was noted for beautiful lawn parties. Lights were strung up, and sawdust was tossed on the ground for people to dance on. The city was full of music.

Mahalia also heard music played for the spectacular funerals that are held to this day only in New Orleans. When somebody who was well loved or respected died, and if he belonged to a secret order such as the Knights of Pythias, the society would hire a band. The mourners would dress in their uniforms and celebrate. "People cried at the incoming of a child and rejoiced at the outgoing," Mahalia said, explaining the philosophy of New Orleans. In the funeral procession, a coffin was set on a wagon drawn by two or four white horses, with men in their uniforms. The band would start playing a sad, holy song, such as "Nearer My God to Thee," or "What a Friend We Have in Jesus," outside a church. Society members marched behind the dead person all the way to the cemetery. When the coffin was buried and the family left, the band, which had been paid to do so, turned around and struck up another song, such as "When the Saints Go Marching In." But now the music was played in an upbeat, jubilant tempo. On the way home from the cemetery, people all along the route would join the procession, singing, dancing, and playing instruments. These people were called the Second Line.

"People would always be happy. The music would do something to them. The music is in my soul," Mahalia said. She compared her feeling to the affection that the Irish and Italians and other people have for folk and religious music from their own cultures. "It's just me," she said of Second Line music. "It's a part of New Orleans people. It's like eating red beans and rice."

She even heard music at home. When Aunt Duke went to work, Mahalia took out a record player that Aunt Duke's son, Freddie, owned. Mahalia played his records, some by blues singers Ma Rainey and Mamie Smith, but especially the ones by Bessie Smith, a very great blues singer called the Empress of the Blues. She had learned from Ma Rainey. Mamie Smith had learned from both of them and had recorded a very popular song called "Crazy Blues" in 1922. That was the record that made record companies decide to put out more African-American music, and these race records, as they were called, were profitable. But Mahalia loved Bessie's voice most of all. She used to sing along with Bessie and try to make her mouth produce the same tones. "Her music haunted you even when she stopped singing," Mahalia would recall with awe.

She spent hours mimicking Bessie, who used many of the musical techniques that people used for church songs. For example, both blues and church singers glided between the notes instead of going directly from one note to another. The technique was called bending the notes. The effect was bluesy and mournful. In those days Mahalia was open-minded about singing the blues. She drank in all the musical influences she could find. She even recalled hearing records by the great Italian opera singer Enrico Caruso played in the white neighborhoods, where she sometimes walked on her way to pick up and drop off laundry loads.

Mahalia also admired the music of a Pentecostal church, which was also called a Sanctified church, in her neighborhood. People shouted and clapped, and they accompanied themselves on instruments, particularly drums, cymbals, tambourines, and steel triangles. Sometimes they became so carried away with their rhythmic shouting, dancing, and stomping that they went into trances or fainted. Aunt Duke forbade Mahalia to go to that church but said she could listen to the music from the steps of her own house. Mahalia fell under the spell of the rhythms and the spirit of the Sanctified church music. She began to put some of that rousing, swinging, exciting feeling into her own songs. She would later realize that a great deal of the music that became popular in the United States and the rest of the world—jazz and rhythm and blues, for example—was based on the rhythms, melodies, and spirit of the Sanctified church.

The highlight of her life was the small Mount Moriah Baptist Church near her house. "Aunt Duke stood for so little play at home that I used to spend all my spare time at the Baptist church," she recalled for *Movin' on Up.* "If you helped scrub it out, they let you help ring the big bell for the early-morning service." There were services every evening, which people respected as much as they did Sunday services. On Saturday nights silent movies were shown in the community room. In the afternoons children sang and played games in the community house in the back of the church. Something was always going on at church.

Mahalia never had a doll from a store; she made her own rag doll and braided grass for the hair. At Christmastime Aunt Duke never had a tree, but the church had lights that delighted Mahalia. And Aunt Duke cooked wonderful food—turkeys, goose, and all kinds of pies, cakes, and bread. Mahalia fell in love with the special foods of New Orleans. She was brought up to believe that good food was important for the strength it gave people, and it was a matter of pride to be a good cook. Her reminiscences of childhood were always filled with descriptions of food.

She learned to love to eat, and that was undoubtedly how she cured herself of the disfiguring rickets by the time she was a teenager. Her family grew its own vegetables and caught fish, crabs, and crayfish in the river. She recalled how families took turtles for soup and baby alligators for meat and sausage from the swamps. A child could sneak up on a baby alligator sunning itself, whack it over the head, and catch it. Mahalia did it. From the woods came raccoons, rabbits, and opossums. People picked peaches, figs, bananas, pecans, and oranges from the trees. New Orleans also had a tradition called "the pan." Whatever white employers had left over from their dinners—not the plate scrapings, but the food left uneaten—was given to the cooks and the maids. The "pan" helped women raise their families on good food.

In one of her published reminiscences of her life, Mahalia gave elaborate instructions about how to get headcheese— the jelly from a pig's head—by boiling it. She also described the way to make hot-water corn bread, done with water, cornmeal, and a little grease, fried and eaten with greens and beans. "When the Negroes were so poor that they couldn't get anything to eat but cornmeal, God's pure water, and the plants that grew in the ground, it kept them going. That's what the old Negro down South grew up on. That's what he cut cotton on—beans, corn bread, greens, and a little syrup," she said—one of her many reveries about the glories of food.

Mahalia learned to love food so much that she would grow up to be a very big woman—two hundred fifty pounds

30

as an adult. Aunt Duke, too, and other women in her family were big women. Despite all her problems with Duke, Mahalia admired her aunt's cooking talent. Mahalia learned from watching Duke in the kitchen.

But most of all, Mahalia found herself drawn to the powerful music and thrilling services at church. "I liked the way the old preacher would preach his message. . . . He had a singing tone in his voice that was sad, and it done something to me," she would recall when she grew up to be famous for singing the gospel. "It is the basic way that I sing today, from hearing the way the preacher would sort of sing, would preach in a cry, in a moan, would . . . chant . . . a groaning sound, which would penetrate to my heart."

When the people in the congregation sang in church, she preferred their tone quality to the somber, quiet songs of the choir. She admired the preachers' devotion to their religious calling. Most of them had to have jobs on the side to keep their families going. Ministers didn't earn salaries from churches in those days; they subsisted on their earnings from other jobs plus any gifts that people in their congregations gave them—chickens, a pair of shoes, or a few pennies in the collection plate.

As Mahalia grew older, she became more church-centered. She would always recognize the value of the blues she had liked as a child. Her people were able to sing about their problems and express themselves spiritually through the woeful tales of their lives set to music. The music with its rhythms and bent notes was usually based on church hymns. Only the words were changed. But Mahalia decided to leave the blues behind. "The blues is some of our finest music," she would say much later in life, when she made an autobiographical tape, *I Sing Because I'm Happy*. "But it doesn't give you any relief. Like a man who drinks, when he's through with his drink, he still has his trouble." Once you got through singing the blues, you still had the blues, she explained.

That was not completely true. People who sang the blues found relief in channeling their unhappiness into music. That was a creative and uplifting activity for them and their audiences. Mahalia knew what good singers were able to do with

31

the blues. "The Negroes all over the South kept these blues playing to take our mind off our burdens," she told a writer, who coauthored her autobiography; excerpts were published in the *Saturday Evening Post* in 1959. But Mahalia needed to lift her mind off her troubles completely. Her belief in God came together with her love of music and the feelings in her heart when she sang church songs.

She sometimes started in a sad vein, but she always ended up in a joyful frame of mind. "Some people were a little ashamed of folk and gospel songs," she discovered as she went along in life, "because it didn't take a lot of studying, and people didn't think that was art, and something that came from the heart was too simple to be accepted. But nobody can hurt the gospel. It's a two-edged sword, no matter if Satan himself can sing a gospel song. I liked to sing 'Jesus, Lover of My Soul,'" she would reflect. "I sing that for myself. Sometimes you feel like you are so far from God, and these deep songs have meaning and bring back the communication between you and God."

Another hymn that she sang beautifully was "His Eye Is On the Sparrow," about how she had no reason to be downcast and defeated, because she knew that God's eye was on the littlest creatures, even the sparrow, and she knew God thought of her, too.

Though she found comfort in the church, Mahalia had very little hope for her happiness in New Orleans. She could sing in church for the love of doing it. But the city offered her few opportunities. Most African-American men worked as long-shoremen, or plasterers and bricklayers. Women had jobs as cooks and maids for a day's pay. That would be her only choice, if she stayed in town.

3

GOING TO CHICAGO

Mahalia never disobeyed her Aunt Duke, but Duke's son, Freddie, was a free spirit. He worked on the docks, but he also dressed in fine clothes and went to speakeasies, where he was friendly with hustlers, musicians, entertainers, sporting men, and party-loving women. He felt at ease in the red-light district and in Storyville, sections of town where parties, gambling, prostitution, and all sorts of vices and high life reigned. Freddie also played the guitar, and he admired Mahalia's talent for singing. He kept telling her to get out of town, perhaps go on the road with him and sing professionally. She adored him, and she didn't blame him for his lifestyle. She was actually proud of him because, no matter how Aunt Duke scolded him, he did exactly as he pleased, and everyone seemed to like him.

"Fred was the only one who could get around Aunt Duke," Mahalia recalled for *Movin' on Up*. "He laughed at her scolding and went his way, and she couldn't do anything about it but love him. He was a great big, jet-black, good-looking man with pearly teeth. . . . I was crazy about him and I was always excited about the life he led."

But one day a horrible message came to Aunt Duke's house. Freddie was dead. He may have been killed in a fight in St. Louis. Mahalia wasn't ever sure exactly how it happened, but her beloved cousin met a violent death. His body was brought back to New Orleans, where the social club he belonged to staged a typical New Orleans funeral for him, with the traditional horse-drawn coffin on a chariot, a marching band, and a Second Line. Mahalia had never felt as sorrowful before as she did about Freddie. She took his death as a sign that she should leave town.

At around that time, she had a serious fight with Aunt Duke, Laurraine Goreau reported in *Just Mahalia, Baby*. Mahalia was known for having a wide, warm smile that could light up a room. She was a girl who loved to laugh with friends. Duke, however, was anything but fun-loving. At one time Duke had been so strict with Mahalia and had beaten her so often with the cat-o'-nine-tails that the neighbors and Mahalia's other aunts became alarmed. They prevailed upon the Snyders, whom Mahalia had worked for, to talk to Duke. Their support may have helped Mahalia for a while, but Duke had a mean streak and was always demanding perfection. She hadn't even given Mahalia permission to be baptized when she reached her teens, saying that Mahalia wasn't ready. But Mahalia had worked and prayed so hard to prepare herself for the big event—baptism in the Mississippi—that the minister and other people in her church and family insisted she was ready. Duke refused to believe them. They joined forces and bought material to sew her white dress for the ceremony. Aunt Duke wasn't convinced until the last moment that Mahalia should be baptized.

Finally Aunt Duke went too far one day. Mahalia wasn't supposed to be out of the house after dark. But walking home with a cousin one late afternoon, she was persuaded to stop at a friend's house where a party was going on. A boy began flirting with Mahalia's cousin and asked her to go to the punch bowl with him. Next thing Mahalia knew, the boy was trying to attack her cousin. While he was wrestling with her in a corner, pulling her clothes off, Mahalia grabbed a knife and stabbed him. The wound was not very deep, but enough to stop the attack. Others at the party tended to his wound while she and her cousin ran away. Mahalia got home after dark. Duke was so furious that she threw Mahalia out of the house. Mahalia went across the street to stay with a neighbor.

The next day she decided she wouldn't go back home. When Aunt Duke was out at work, Mahalia, unwilling to let herself be abused anymore, went to get her things. Within a few days the neighbors helped her find a house for rent at six dollars a month. From the door, she could see the Mount Moriah Baptist Church a block and a half away. She could see Aunt Duke's house, too.

Mahalia didn't really have enough money to strike out on her own. But she was earning a few dollars a week as a laundress, and she was determined to make ends meet. One cousin gave her a stove. Somebody else supplied a bed. Although everyone worried about her, somehow she kept going. By this time, Duke wanted her back, but Mahalia refused to go. The neighbors reminded Duke that she had thrown Mahalia out.

Duke's husband had gone to Chicago and had come back with tales of how black people could ride on streetcars with whites, shop in their stores, and mix with them. Even Mahalia's father had gone, though he had come back with discouraging stories about Chicago's cold weather and rushing people. He was even afraid that gangsters there would kill him. But from many people Mahalia had been hearing about the opportunities for African-Americans in Chicago since she was a little girl. "I finally began to have this longing desire to go up to Chicago and see for myself. The last thing at night before I went to sleep I would whisper to my pillow that someday the sun was going to shine down on me in Chicago."

Aunt Hannah, another of her mother's six sisters, came down from Chicago to visit the family for Thanksgiving in 1927. Hannah, who had always been adventurous, had moved to Chicago permanently. When she was getting ready to go back, Mahalia decided to accompany her. Aunt Duke argued with the teenager, telling her that her life would become a vale of trouble without the church nearby. Mahalia had no such worries. "I was almost a young woman, tall and strong as an ox with a will of my own," she assessed herself. She made up her mind to go to Chicago and study nursing.

She ran to the train station, where she found a redcap who sold her the return portion of a discount excursion ticket for four dollars. And she and Hannah packed a big basket of chicken, pies, and sandwiches to sustain them, got into their coach seats on a segregated train, and rode for two nights and a day sitting up, while the train went up the country. "I never dreamed then that trains had beds or dining cars," Mahalia remembered about her first long-distance train trip. Trying to take every precaution with her money, she traveled with one hundred dollars pinned to her bra. The money was her life's savings from work as a nursemaid and laundress in New Orleans.

When she got off the train, the wind was blowing the snow around. She was astounded when her aunt waved to a white cabdriver and he stopped for them. Hannah explained that the driver was happy to have the women ride in his cab. It was a business arrangement. To Mahalia, it seemed like a miracle. But the cold weather in Chicago shocked her. She didn't have any heavy clothes.

For about a week she stayed in an apartment with Hannah and another aunt, Alice, and Alice's children on Prairie Avenue on the South Side, which had become an African-American community. The aunts found a place for Mahalia to sleep in the room with her young cousins. And Mahalia spent time trying to get up the courage to start building a life in this cold northern city, which was noisy and crowded, with big, frightening buildings.

Alice found her a job not far from hers in a white family's house. Every morning they traveled on the same elevated train to work, and at night they met at the train station and rode back to the South Side ghetto. It was Mahalia's plan to save enough money to go to nursing school. But then her Aunt Hannah fell ill from asthma and a heart ailment, and Mahalia and Alice became the sole support of the family. Not only did

Mahalia have to pay for her own room and her share of the food, but she had to work simply to help all of them survive. So she was still doing laundry for white people. "It was all I knew how to do," she said in *Movin' on Up*. She wasn't able to save money to go to school.

For a while, even though she was unable to afford a warm coat, she got up every day at 6:00 A.M. to travel to work on the elevated train. Shivering in the cold, wearing sweatshirts and sweaters, watching the snow blow around as the sun started to rise, she sometimes felt low, lonely, and afraid.

The burdens of life in Chicago became easier for her, though, when Alice took her to the Greater Salem Baptist Church in the neighborhood. The first time Mahalia showed up for choir rehearsal, hoping to be allowed to sing in the choir of about fifty people, she sang so loud that the choir director stopped everyone. "I was ready to die—I was so sure he was going to put me out," Mahalia recalled. Instead he asked her to sing alone. She prayed that she could get through the song. She chose "Hand Me Down My Silver Trumpet, Gabriel," which she knew well from New Orleans. Afterward the choir director told her she was going to be a soloist. She was delighted.

Chicago had its glamorous side that fascinated her, too. She noticed that African-Americans had created a lively, prospering community for themselves. They had foundations and clubs, and doctors, dentists, ministers, aldermen, policemen, firemen, teachers, and lawyers. Churchpeople talked about getting educated. People had ambitions. She admired the ones who had started their own businesses. It could be a simple ham hock business or a beauty salon, but a business gave a person a feeling of independence and control in life, she thought. She felt inspired to want to start a business of her own one day.

She loved to go to Michigan Avenue and look at people dressed in fine clothes—men with cream-colored spats, derbies, and walking sticks, and women in fur coats leading little dogs on leashes, going to theaters, clubs, and restaurants and driving Rolls Royces. Some people had prospered in real estate and in the insurance business. The South Side was the second-largest Negro community in the world, she knew, second only to Harlem in New York: "You could go for miles and miles on the South Side, between Eighteenth Street and Fifty-fifth Street, from the stockyards on the west to the white neighborhoods along the shore of Lake Michigan to the east, without seeing a white person."

Many New Orleans jazz musicians came to Chicago to play—among them Louis Armstrong and, pianist Earl Hines who was a star leading a band at the Grand Terrace Ballroom. They would soon hear Mahalia's voice when she sang in church, and they would ask her to perform with them. But she would refuse and keep singing only in churches and for religious ceremonies and events. Nevertheless in her first days in Chicago, she viewed all the sights with feelings of wonder and admiration for the achievements of her own people. "I stood in line to hear Bessie Smith at the Avenue Theater and sat in my seat so thrilled to hear her as she filled the whole place with her voice that I never went home until they put us out and closed up for the night," she wrote in *Movin' on Up*.

She frequently went to church on weeknights after working as a maid all day, and she became friends with other gospel singers in the church. Soon she was singing in a gospel group known as the Johnson Brothers, with Robert Johnson, his boogie-woogie-playing pianist brother Prince, another brother, Wilbur, and a singer named Louise Barry. The Johnson Brothers were sons of the minister who had founded the Greater Salem Baptist Church. They sang in other churches, too, making the rounds for all sorts of services and events, sometimes earning as much as $1.50 each a night. Many nights, when she wasn't singing, Mahalia got off the train after her days as a laundress and went to the church simply to visit with her new friends. Her life filled up with church services, socials, and picnics. The Johnson family became as close as relatives to her. She stopped feeling homesick for New Orleans.

"There's an awful lot of Negro churches in Chicago—and you don't catch any of them empty on Sunday. So my singing in churches made me known," she would reminisce about her early days in Chicago in the 1920s and 1930s. "My singing was getting better, too, and I was beginning to get a little money from it. Sometimes I got ten dollars a week singing at churches and for funerals," she said for her book *Movin' on Up*, published in 1966.

The Johnson Brothers began to get invitations to travel outside of Chicago. Because the brothers weren't always eager to leave Chicago, Mahalia sometimes struck out on her own, traveling on the "gospel highway" alone, singing at Baptist churches all around the country. There was no actual highway, of course. That was just a figure of speech. Gospel singing was becoming increasingly popular with African-American churchgoers, and gospel singers moved around the country to perform as guests in churches far from their homes. Talented singing groups banded together with all sorts of entertainers and traveled to churches to perform. The traveling groups were big enough sometimes to amount to little caravans. When Mahalia traveled alone, ministers passed her along, paving the way for her to travel safely from one church and one town to the next.

In the beginning, she sometimes earned a nickel for every person who came to hear her, both in Chicago and on the road. Other times the ministers passed the collection plate and shared the contributions with her. That way she often earned about $1.50, whether she was appearing with the Johnson Brothers or on her own. Sometimes she arrived in a town to find that her performance had been canceled. But she kept going on to the next town, with ministers smoothing the way for her, arranging for her to stay at their houses and eat with them, deducting her room and board from her fees when she was paid. Then she was on her way again. It was a hard life, but gospel singers kept their sense of humor, saying that they traveled along the gospel highway on "maypop tires"—weak and worn old tires that "may pop at any minute."

When she sang in Chicago, a friend cut tickets out of cardboard used by the laundries to make shirts stiff. The cost of admission to her performances began at a nickel per person, went up to ten cents, then to a quarter. Mahalia would always recall a kind gospel performance producer who arranged for her to sing in the Ebenezer Baptist Church in Chicago and raised her price to forty cents. Mahalia sometimes drove around town herself and put up cardboard signs announcing her upcoming performances. She knew that the wealthier African-Americans in the bigger Baptist churches laughed at her simple promotion activities. They and their ministers didn't approve of her spirited, down-home southern style of singing. They especially disliked the way she danced in the aisles, shook her body, and fell to her knees, behaving as if she was a bit possessed. But Mahalia didn't let herself become discouraged. She felt that the Lord was hoping for her to succeed. She began to wear robes instead of the street clothes that could reveal her body too much as she moved around excitedly. Some people with a sense of humor would recall that Mahalia was the sexiest of all the gospel singers. Later on she would say that she always felt like a peacock in full plumage when she sang and danced, overcome by religious fervor.

She alternated between working as a "fish-and-bread" gospel singer on the road and staying home to earn $7.50 a week steadily as a laundress in Chicago and to sing in churches there. But she was so often gone from Chicago that she lost her laundress jobs. Once she took a job as a date packer on an assembly line in a factory because the pay was more than double what she earned as a maid. But she couldn't stand repeating the same motion all day long, putting dates in boxes. It was driving her crazy. Fights broke out among the other women workers. When they pulled knives on each other, she became terrified and quit the job.

By 1929, Chicago had changed. The Depression came to the South Side, as it did to the rest of the country. Banks closed, and people wandered around, crying over their lost savings. Their fine clothes began to look shabby. Those who had driven fancy cars to theaters began hustling for their living as jitney drivers. And some of them had to give up their cars. The jitneys competed with buses until the bus companies started hiring African-American drivers. Mansions on Michigan Avenue were turned into tiny apartments, with crowds of people sharing one kitchen. Many people became homeless, slept on newspapers in alleys, and had nothing to eat. Mahalia thought it might have been easier to go through the Depression in New Orleans, where people could at least grow their own food or fish in the Mississippi.

She saw riots start in the streets when people protested their evictions before the New Deal of President Franklin Delano Roosevelt. He began to create jobs for people on public works projects under the National Recovery Act. But before that happened, Chicago turned into a grim and somber city. It broke Mahalia's heart to see the ruin of people's hopes and dreams. Gambling became more entrenched than ever in a city where people had always liked to bet. All kinds of businesses sprang up as fronts for gambling parlors. In the back of a delicatessen with a few cans of food, a person could pass through a hidden doorway into a gambling game in a backroom. The numbers games became more popular than ever.

"If you earned a dollar, you felt guilty about spending it on yourself," Mahalia would eventually tell many writers.

One day Mahalia had the good fortune to earn $1.75. On her way home she passed a group of people waiting in a breadline. "I fished the money out of my pocket and told them to follow me. We bought a sack of potatoes and a mess of smoked ribs and took it all back to my place and had one big supper, all of us." Later she would reflect on how happy it always made her to cook meals for a big crowd of people. "A good meal seems to bring a warm feeling of harmony among people. You begin eating and laughing, and time goes by, and you realize that you've had a pleasant time together, and the day seems bright to you," she wrote in *Movin' on Up*.

THE LONG CLIMB UP TO $1,000
FOR A SINGLE NIGHT

Oddly enough, the Depression gave Mahalia's gospel-singing vocation a boost. Churches had to charge little admission fees to pay for the costs of coal and mortgages, and the ministers gave the remaining money to gospel groups such as the Johnson Brothers. The singers were the attraction that lured people into the churches and kept the doors open. Gospel singers would become more numerous; they would start to make recordings, and their reputations would spread. By the early 1940s, a golden age of gospel would begin and last for nearly two decades.

Because Mahalia didn't make a living as a gospel singer in the early 1930s, she found a job as a hotel maid for twelve dollars a week. That job kept her in Chicago on a fairly steady basis. She saved every penny she could and didn't mind curtailing her travels. For one thing, she appreciated the weekly salary from the hotel, and sometimes her singing in churches and at funerals brought her ten dollars a week. Mahalia was among the most active of the gospel singers, and her voice started to become familiar. Children, some of whom would later become famous as jazz musicians, heard Mahalia sing in those days. "She sang all around town," recalled Joe Williams, a great jazz singer raised in Chicago, who started earning an international reputation when he joined Count Basie's band in the 1950s.

"Gospel music in those days of the early 1930s was really taking wing," Mahalia wrote in *Movin' on Up*. "It was the kind of music colored people had left behind them down South and they liked it because it was just like a letter from home."

Moving around in the gospel world, meeting other singers, she met a man named Thomas A. Dorsey when she attended Baptist conventions. He would become one of the most highly regarded composers of gospel hymns. The song that made him especially famous was "Precious Lord, Take My Hand." Among his many other well-loved hymns were "I'm Going to Live the Life I Sing About in My Song" and "It Doesn't Cost Very Much."

Dorsey had lived a colorful life. As a child he had fallen in love with the music of the Baptist church, as Mahalia had done. But he switched direction and became a professional blues singer and boogie-woogie piano player, writing sexy blues songs and accompanying Ma Rainey, a well-known early blues artist. Eventually Dorsey became attracted to the church again and left his career as a bluesman.

An enterprising businessman, he took along sheet-music copies of his hymns and sold them for a few cents apiece as he traveled on the gospel highway. He began traveling with Mahalia, who watched in fascination when he sold so many copies that he prospered. She remained a fish-and-bread singer, she called herself, singing for her supper. She used up most of her earnings as a maid and singer to survive, paying room and board to Aunt Hannah. But Mahalia admired Dorsey's many talents. In those days, which were the heyday of gospel music, the gospel repertoire was growing. Mahalia sang older gospel songs—hymns dating back to the nineteenth century called "Dr. Watts hymns," named for a long-ago composer—and spirituals that had come out of the

43

folk tradition. A well-loved Dr. Watts hymn is "The Day Is Past and Gone," about the coming of death. And one of the most famous hymns in the Dr. Watts tradition is "Amazing Grace," written by John Newton, a onetime slave ship captain. The version that African-Americans sing contains the words:

> *Through many dangers, toils and snares,*
> *I have already come.*
> *'Twas grace that brought me safe thus far*
> *And grace will lead me home.*

But in the twentieth century, new composers came along, writing hymns of equal merit to those of Dr. Isaac Watts. Among the best new composers of gospel songs were Dorsey, C. A. Tindley, and Herbert Brewster. Mahalia was not a composer herself, but Dorsey wrote some songs for her because he found her way of singing them so compelling.

Even before Dorsey worked with Mahalia, he had heard her and the Johnson Brothers singing in churches, particularly in the storefronts popular with new settlers from the South. He had admired the teenager for her outgoing personality in a crowd. It made her an ideal person to become popular in the gospel world, where the church was the center of African-American community life. She knew how to assert herself and win the respect of many, though at first not all, preachers and fellow Baptists. "She was a good mixer . . . and she loved everybody, at least she acted like she loved everybody. She called everybody 'baby, honey, darling.'. . . She made a wonderful [impression]," Dorsey said in *The Rise of Gospel Blues* by Michael W. Harris. Dorsey recalled her as the only woman in the Johnson Brothers group, which was "really rocking them everywhere they went. Mahalia was with this group and was going and killing them off. I mean she was laying them out," he said, describing her power over audiences. He also knew that the Johnson Brothers offended the conservative people in old-line churches. One pastor told them to get that "jazz" out of his church. Mahalia called back to him, "This is the way we sing down south." But Dorsey observed that she became popular exactly because of her emotional style of singing. Her warmth and spirit brought southern traditions to the north and made life easier for homesick newcomers like herself, reminding them of the tightly knit, church-centered communities filled with relatives they had left behind.

Dorsey tried to give her advice about her technique, but Mahalia preferred to do whatever she wanted. She once went along with a girlfriend, also a singer, who suggested she take a lesson with a trained singer, Professor Dubois, on the South Side. He criticized Mahalia's singing style unmercifully. He thought she sang too loudly, and her pronunciation of words didn't measure up to his standards. He disliked her untutored, exuberant style, too, and told her she was an embarrassment to the Negro People. Mahalia was very hurt. She never went to anyone for another lesson. When she was asked about her style, she said she sang the way she felt, the way she had always sung, having learned her hymns and deepened her belief as a child in New Orleans. That was the way the best gospel singers had always learned their art. Their emotional style had already instructed and inspired blues and jazz singers, and all the most popular music styles—rock and roll, and rhythm and blues—to come along by the 1950s would have their roots in the soulfulness and naturalness of the gospel tradition. Audiences loved her, and that was good enough for her.

Mahalia had a second good reason to stay in Chicago with her hotel job and church dates. She had met a handsome, tall, dark man named Isaac Hockenhull, who was called Ike, at a church social in 1935. Ten years older than she, he seemed to be a very serious, educated man. He had a degree in chemistry from Tuskegee Institute in the South. He also had a lovely speaking voice that captivated her. Because of the Depression, he couldn't find a job at his level of education, and so he had gone to work in the post office. She couldn't believe that Ike Hockenhull could have a serious interest in her, a young woman who had left school in the eighth grade. But he was in love with her and with her voice;

he went to all of her performances. Mahalia reckoned that they had known each other for a year by the time he persuaded her to marry him. The ceremony took place in her Aunt Hannah's apartment, where the couple lived for a while until they found an apartment of their own.

Ike's mother had run a cosmetics business before the Depression, but she had lost all her money. Ike, who had helped his mother mix creams and lotions, still knew the formulas. He and Mahalia sometimes stayed up all night concocting cosmetics to sell on the side. Ike took bottles along on his mail route to sell to women. Mahalia packed cosmetics into a bag to take with her on the gospel highway, where she sold them outside of churches. The money they earned could have helped Mahalia and Ike live at a higher level. Mahalia was excellent at saving money. But she soon found out that Ike loved to gamble on the horse races. He was nearly as devoted to the racetrack as she was to her gospel singing.

Then there came a day when Ike lost his job at the post office. At the same time, Mahalia found her job at the hotel was gone when she came back from a singing date out of town. Ike discovered that an audition was being held for a singer to play in *The Hot Mikado*, a jazz version of Gilbert and Sullivan's operetta *The Mikado*. He argued with Mahalia, as he had done so many times, that she shouldn't waste her gorgeous voice on gospel music when she could sing the blues or jazz and become a highly paid entertainer. Mahalia told him, as usual, that she couldn't stand to sing anything but gospel songs. She had to believe in the songs she sang. The focus of her life was her belief in God. She didn't want to sing about sad, hard times. Ike reminded her that both of them were down to their last dollars. "That theater work will pay you sixty dollars a week," he told her. "I'm going out to find work. You've got to do the same."

"Some people smile when I tell them that afternoon was one of the most painful in my whole life," Mahalia wrote in *Movin' on Up*. She was terribly depressed at the thought of the audition. When she got to the Great Northern Theater downtown, a white woman on duty inside told her, "You have to bring copies of the songs you want to sing." Mahalia had a book called *Gospel Pearls*. The woman said those songs wouldn't do. Mahalia went out to a sheet-music store and browsed until she found the spiritual "Sometimes I Feel Like a Motherless Child." "Somebody had gone and arranged it and stuck their name on a big piece of sheet music," she said. She bought it and went back to the audition, where she took a seat and kept hoping they would never call her. Perhaps they would hire one of the other girls before they had time to listen to her. But she was called; the people in charge of the audition were listening to everyone.

The pianist took the sheet music and began to play it. Mahalia had never heard the arrangement before and let the pianist run though it completely. When he started a second time, she began to sing. "Nobody could have sung 'Sometimes I Feel Like a Motherless Child' the way I did. I didn't have to put it on. I felt lost and deserted. When I got through, you could hear a pin drop. Finally one of the judges said, 'Why didn't you start to sing when the song was played for you the first time?'"

"Because I never heard it played that way before," she said.

The piano player told her that he had played it exactly the way it was written on the sheet, but Mahalia just shrugged and didn't bother to tell him that she couldn't read music.

She left the theater and wandered around, postponing her trip home. When she got there, she found Ike in an unusual state of excitement. He had just had a phone call from the theater. She had won the part at the audition. And he had gotten a job, too. She said, "You got a job! Then that settles it. Then I don't have to sing in that show. I'm not going to any rehearsal. I'm quitting right now!"

Ike argued with her; he was furious. But Mahalia stood her ground. That disagreement was a turning point in their relationship. He knew that she would never agree to become an entertainer. She might spend the rest of her life as a fish-and-bread singer. Mahalia, for her part, would soon admit to herself that Ike would never give up his addiction to betting on the horses. Sometimes he won a lot of money. But sometimes he lost a lot.

One day he won thousands of dollars at the track, and he gave her the money to keep for them. She was going out of town to sing, so she put the money, laid out bill by bill, under a rug. But when she came back and lifted the rug, she found that all the money was gone. He had found it and spent it on the horses.

Ike was a good man—but incorrigible. He himself said that Mahalia couldn't stand their lifestyle—one day chicken, next day feathers. But he was helpless to stop gambling.

Mahalia, who had never been able to afford to become a nurse, turned her attention to opening a beauty salon. She couldn't afford to go to beautician's school and get a state–required license. So she rented a storefront—probably for about twenty-five dollars a month in the Depression days—hired a licensed beautician, and got down on her hands and knees to scrub the shop and make it sparkle. Soon Mahalia's Beauty Salon was so busy that she had to hire more people—relatives and friends, who kept the shop going when she left town to sing. Always fired by ambition to be a successful businesswoman, and with the self-confidence never to shrink from a challenge, she then opened a florist's shop called Mahalia's House of Flowers. In some versions of the story, she said that people were always asking her to sing at funerals, and they wouldn't buy flowers from her shop unless she promised to sing. "They didn't care how the flowers looked, just so I was there to sing," she said in *Movin' on Up*. But in Laurraine Goreau's book *Just Mahalia, Baby*, Mahalia told people that they had to buy flowers from her shop if they wanted her to sing at funerals and other church events. They bought flowers from her because they wanted her glorious voice to grace their services.

In either case, she was prospering. When she traveled, she pinned money to her underclothes. Sometimes she gave Ike money to pay off his gambling debts. He had occasional jobs, but nothing turned out to be steady for him.

They still had some good times together, though. Childless, they unofficially adopted a boy. He was a southern-born child whose mother had abandoned him when he was five years old. She had given him to a couple who ran a sporting house —a house of prostitution—in Mississippi. The little boy ran errands for the couple, and he helped clean their place, too. In return he had a roof over his head and food to eat. The couple was a poor substitute for a family, but they were all the little boy had. It isn't clear if Mahalia met him when she was touring in Mississippi or when he came to live in Chicago after being rescued by his Aunt Carrie. But Mahalia did meet the boy in the 1930s. His name was John Sellers. He started to visit Mahalia all the time at her beauty salon, because he was desperately in need of affection. His Aunt Carrie, who had taken him from the sporting house down south, turned out to be as cold as his mother. John actually missed the woman who ran the sporting house, because she had paid attention to him, even though she had forced him to work as a handyman. Carrie, who worked as a maid for a Chicago gangster, went to church all the time and was supposed to be a good Christian woman. But she let Mahalia know that she didn't have any room in her heart or her apartment for little John. Mahalia said the boy could come to live with her and Ike.

Ike turned out to be a very good, affectionate stepfather who took time to talk and play with the boy. At first John slept in the same bed with Ike and Mahalia, since there was no other bed in the apartment. Then they acquired a cot on which John settled down. The living arrangement didn't last forever. Young as he was, John found a job working for a white couple who wanted him to look after their apartment, and they found him a private apartment nearby and gave him lovely presents. So he moved into his own place happily before he was a teenager. But he kept going to see Ike and Mahalia, who were the closest thing to a real family that he ever had.

Mahalia discovered that John could sing very well. She began to take him with her to gospel performances, where he was called Little Brother John Sellers. Sometimes she sent him to sing in her place, if she didn't feel like going for one reason or another, or if she had two singing dates scheduled for the same time. Mahalia's sponsorship launched John's career as a singer. Later on, when she became famous, he and Mahalia began to fight and to find fault with each other. He thought she became conceited and stingy with money because of her fame. But he would never forget how she had loved him when he was a homeless, unwanted child.

At around this time, a friend advised her to buy a house with six apartments in it. She was already very busy with the beauty salon, the flower shop, and her singing career. She didn't have to work a single day as a maid anymore. At first she was reluctant to invest in a house, but she prayed all one night to have an answer from the Lord about what she should do. The spirit of the Lord answered her, convincing her that she should buy the building. She went ahead; the building brought her income. Her lack of schooling never hampered her ability to do mathematics, keep track of money, and turn a profit from her ventures. She knew how to save a penny and use it to her advantage—if Ike didn't spend it.

The showdown for her marriage to Ike came at around this time, probably because of his gambling. After she had worked very hard to bring home some money, he told her that he had lost a great deal of money; it had been stolen, he said, and it wasn't just his own money, but insurance premiums belonging to other people, too, according to Laurraine Goreau. Mahalia gave him all her money to keep him out of trouble. But she threw him out of the house on that cold, snowy night. In the morning he was still outside the door. He loved and needed her. He didn't want to leave. But she decided that it was time for them to separate. He was ruining her.

It would take them a long time to get a divorce; they always remained friends. Mahalia would often give him a check when he came to her in need of money. He didn't live very far from her. When friends asked her if she felt ashamed of being divorced, she said no; the Lord had guided her to give up on her marriage.

Her life revolved around work; she was loyal above all to her gospel singing. She had learned to take care of herself very well at home and on the road.

Once, she was booked to sing in Philadelphia by a gospel promoter. When she showed up, he told her the performance was scheduled for the next night. He said she could sing instead the first night at an auditorium in Newark, New Jersey. So she went there and found out that a great deal of publicity had advertised her performance well in advance. She figured out that it had been no mistake about the date. The promoter in Philadelphia had booked her for one night and, without telling her, had arranged to subcontract her for the previous night to the promoter in Newark. Tickets had been sold. Mahalia demanded that she get paid that very minute or she wouldn't sing, and the audience would tear the auditorium down. So the promoter in Newark paid her.

When she went back to Philadelphia, the original promoter asked her for his share of the money. She refused to give anything to him. He wasn't entitled to a share, she said. She had done the traveling and singing. He pulled a gun on her. She left quickly and moved into a hotel. The next day the police went to get her. At the station, she had to talk for a long while to make people understand what had happened. The promoter lost all his credibility in the gospel world, and Mahalia kept all the money. She had been successful in protecting her interests.

There were honest promoters, and there were dishonest ones, she knew well. She was meeting all kinds.

When she went on the road, she often took friends and gospel colleagues along with her, sometimes people as illustrious as the great Baptist minister and gospel singer Reverend James Cleveland. He was called her protégé in those days. Little Brother John Sellers went, too. And Robert Anderson, a popular gospel singer in his own right, sometimes accompanied her when she sang. She needed to hire an accompanist. Since her fees were going up, she could afford to.

One day in 1946 she went to sing in Detroit, Michigan, at the church of her friend, the Reverend Clarence L. Franklin, a Baptist preacher who was becoming known nationwide because of his emotionally stirring sermons broadcast on radio. He was a great advocate of self-help. He said that people must believe in themselves and the Lord and work hard to carve out their own destiny. His daughter Aretha, then only four years old, was already singing the gospel in church, showing off a talent she shared with her mother and an older sister. Mahalia was surprised when Johnny Meyers, a famous gospel promoter visiting from New York, asked her if she would like to perform at the Golden Gate Auditorium in Harlem. Many eminent jazz musicians, Duke Ellington among them, entertained there. So did the best gospel performers. For them, the Golden Gate was a mecca, a kind of Metropolitan Opera House. Mahalia said yes.

In New York, she found men wearing sandwich boards promoting her on the street. On the boards, which the men wore slung over their shoulders and hanging down over their chests and backs, were advertisements for her performance. That night the show was sold out. She earned one thousand dollars for herself. Johnny Meyers paid her in cash. When she went back to her hotel room, she kept counting the money. "Look at that!" she said to a friend. "Know how long it been taking Halie to get that much together at once? Let's count it again."

5

MAHALIA GETS A RECORDING CONTRACT AND A PRESTIGIOUS INVITATION AND GIVES A CONCERT AT CARNEGIE HALL

The next morning Johnny Meyers took Mahalia to the studios of Apollo Records, owned by Bess Berman, in New York City. Mrs. Berman, a stocky little woman, was recording African-American performers for the blues and jazz market. Though she had started recording ethnic and folk music, she hadn't yet entered the gospel field. She studied Mahalia while the big woman sang, with her almond-shaped eyes closed and a few strands of her glossy upswept hair coming loose. Mrs. Berman didn't know a thing about gospel music, and so she suggested that Mahalia record a blues number. Mahalia delivered her usual sermon about the blues being the music of despair while the gospel had the magic of the cure. Mrs. Berman thought it over and said, "All right, we'll try you."

(This was not Mahalia's first experience in a recording studio. In 1937, she had been invited to record four songs for Decca, when the company's artists and repertoire man, J. Mayo Williams, heard her singing at a religious service in Chicago. She was so naive about the recording industry at that time that she asked him how much he would charge her. He laughed and told her it was free. She probably wasn't paid much, if anything, for the recordings, either. Little Brother John Sellers went to the studio with her in Chicago, heard her record "God's Gonna Separate the Wheat from the Tares" and "You Sing on, My Singer," accompanied by a piano, and then "God Shall Wipe Away All Tears" and "Keep Me Every Day," with an organ. She may have been the first gospel singer to record with a piano for accompaniment. After the session, Little Brother John recalled, she didn't think she had done a good-enough job. They went to a barbecue restaurant, where she had enough money to buy one soda pop for him and one helping of ribs that she divided between them. She had even saved some ribs for Ike Hockenhull. The recordings managed to get to a bar in her old Pinching Town neighborhood in New Orleans. Everyone she knew showed up to hear them. People screamed about how great her voice was. Even her father went to hear her. For once, he was thrilled to tell everyone in sight: "That's my daughter!")

Bess offered a contract; Mahalia worked out the details. Jules Schwerin, who wrote *Got to Tell It*, a book about Mahalia, said the contract guaranteed Mahalia ten thousand dollars a year. And she decided to record "I'm Going to Tell God All About It One of These Days" as her first song, with "Wait Till My Change Comes" on the flip side. The second record she made for Apollo had the hymns "I Want to Rest" and "He Knows My Heart." Then Mrs. Berman told agent Harry Lenetska, a friend of hers who had handled many talented white and African-American celebrities, to go hear Mahalia sing in a church.

Lenetska fell in love with her voice and believed she could become a star. He invited her to have dinner at his house and meet his family. Mahalia was wary; she had never had an agent in her life. Lenetska told her he would book her for appearances in theaters that would pay ten thousand dollars. Mahalia was skeptical about that, too. "I don't even go in no theater," she told him. She had actually given up going to theaters because she had promised the Lord that she would do so if he would only let her "grandfather" live. He was her uncle Emmanuel, Paul's elderly father, and he had collapsed from a stroke when she insisted he make a special trip to a shop to have a photograph taken on a very hot day while he was visiting her in Chicago. He was rushed to a hospital, where he nearly died. When he survived, she kept her word to the Lord and never stepped inside a theater again. She and Lenetska ended up agreeing to work together in a loose arrangement without a contract and without theaters.

Mahalia's records didn't sell well, and she kept singing solely for church audiences. Nevertheless, the recordings alerted one very important man to her existence. Studs Terkel, a white journalist who had a radio show on WENR in Chicago, was passing by a record store one day when he heard a record by her. He asked who the singer was, then traced her through his connections in the churches. Finding her, he invited her to appear as a guest on his show. He played her first recording so often for audiences that he almost wore it out. "There's a woman on the South Side with a golden voice," he told people, as Laurraine Goreau wrote in her book.

Back in New York, Bess Berman was much less enthusiastic. Mahalia's records failed to attract buyers. Mrs. Berman had to be talked into letting Mahalia record one more song—just one more, an Apollo recording engineer requested. If it didn't sell, then the label could drop Mahalia.

By this time, Mahalia needed a new accompanist who would stay with her all the time. Friends in the gospel world rallied around her and introduced her to a woman named Mildred Falls, a devout Baptist who could play both piano and organ. She was talented in music and experienced in life. She had been married and divorced, and she had seen something of the world, having traveled to California.

Mildred, a big woman like Mahalia, was northern-born, and she would have trouble tolerating the inhumane conditions of segregation when she traveled in the South. But Mildred was a good accompanist, who knew how to swing and play exactly the right music at the moment Mahalia needed support, and when to stop playing and give Mahalia space. The women developed a very close working relationship. Mildred understood Mahalia's style. Their music together was brilliant and exciting. They stayed together for about twenty years.

Right away they began traveling around the country, and they made Mahalia's third recording. The legend is that Mahalia was practicing backstage for a concert, possibly at the Golden Gate in New York, when she started singing an old spiritual. In some versions of the story, Johnny Meyers overheard her. He asked her, "What's that you're singing, Mahalia?"

She said, "Why, it's an old song. I've always sung it, since I was a little child in New Orleans."

He said, "You sing it just right. Why don't you make a record of it?"

So she decided to do that one, "Movin' on Up," for Apollo. Her voice was bell clear, with sunny soprano notes in the pretty melody and a blues tonality especially at the beginning of the song. Here was a bright example of how much the blues and gospel could sound alike and even have a trace of pop music. All around the country people began buying the record. Nothing like it had ever happened in the gospel field before. According to Laurraine Goreau, fifty thousand copies sold in Chicago in one week. The little Apollo label couldn't keep up with demands coming in from all over the country.

At that time, Mahalia was appointed official soloist of the National Baptist Convention, a leading Baptist organization in the country, with about four million members. She was also chosen as the treasurer of its music department. "I not only raise money, but hold it for them, too," she would later tell newspaper reporters. They loved writing about her, because she spoke her mind forthrightly and delivered her witty and perceptive opinions without apology or fear. In the long run, the record "Movin' on Up" sold about two million copies in the United States. But right away it sold at least half a million copies—a roaring success for a record in those days. Jules Schwerin wrote that Mahalia earned *more* than three hundred thousand dollars in royalties in one year. That record made her truly famous, if still only in the African-American communities.

Naturally Mrs. Berman was eager to make more recordings with Mahalia. "Even Me" and "What Could I Do?" sold very well, perhaps as many as a million copies, followed by the best-selling "Dig a Little Deeper" and "Silent Night" and others. Some people close to Mahalia told of fights eventually arising between her and Mrs. Berman about contract terms and the sum of money Mahalia was owed. Mahalia was a diva of the gospel field, and Mrs. Berman was a businesswoman. At one point Mahalia had fifty-eight thousand dollars in cash in a dresser drawer. So she was doing very well, whatever she was actually owed from her performances and recordings.

In New York in March 1949, a pioneering French jazz critic named Hugues Panassie, one of the first serious critics of jazz, visited from Paris and let Mrs. Berman know how much he loved Mahalia's recordings. He took them back to France with him, including Mahalia's version of the beloved old hymn "Amazing Grace," and "In My Home over There." Panassie played these recordings on his radio show. The broadcasts reached England and other countries in Western Europe. The songs were so popular that a company called Vogue, which released Apollo recordings in France and England, decided to distribute Mahalia's work there. Apollo was now one of the big gospel labels on the East Coast of the United States. Though other singers were becoming well known—Roberta Martin, for one, among at least a dozen others—Mahalia was Apollo's most popular star.

She had more things to think about than just her own career. She didn't approve of Little Brother John Sellers, who was now singing the blues at the Apollo Theater in New York. And she had a boyfriend who worked as a barber in Chicago. She was lonely for a man in her life, she said, and even toyed with the idea of having her friend manage her career. But she was really swept up in work. Recording again at the Apollo studios, she met Joe Bostic, a well-known African-

American journalist, producer, and man about town in the entertainment world in New York. Very impressed with her voice, he decided to start booking her to play in African-American churches. But he had other things in mind for her, too.

And from New York came an invitation from Joe Bostic, a former editor of the *Amsterdam News*, an African-American paper, and a concert producer: "Would she give a concert at Carnegie Hall?" she recalled in *Movin' on Up*. That invitation made her head swim. Among churchgoing Baptists, Mahalia had become so famous as a wonderful singer with the power to spread the deep, spiritual, emotional messages of the gospel that it was surely time to bring her into New York's Carnegie Hall where white people, too, could hear her. Some were becoming sufficiently curious about this hidden treasure of the heartland. Walter Winchell, then the most famous columnist in the country, with a very energetic, shouting manner of talking on his radio show, gave Mahalia an outrageous compliment, calling her "the world's greatest gospel canary!"

Terrified at the idea of the concert and, according to some people, at first reluctant to do it, she finally agreed to sing at Carnegie Hall in October 1950. Actually the idea of singing in Carnegie Hall, where so many great singers had performed, excited her. She could not resist or refuse the honor. She did everything she could to cooperate with the people who were producing the concert. But both she and Mildred Falls may have vomited from stage fright just before the performance. Nevertheless, they were a great success. They would soon begin traveling the world, too, and kings and queens and prime ministers became enthralled.

Mahalia was not the only gospel singer to perform at Carnegie Hall that evening in 1950. She shared the stage with Sister Rosetta Tharpe, the Gaye Sisters, and Clara Ward. Each of them had prestige and a following in the gospel world. Ward was particularly inspirational for such budding gospel stars as Aretha Franklin, who would become a rhythm and blues superstar and a top-selling gospel recording artist about twenty years later. But Mahalia was the featured star of the Carnegie Hall concert. She had the voice and the charisma to communicate across all cultural boundaries.

"They said afterward that the critics who went to the concert that night thought they'd got caught in a Cecil B. DeMille mob scene—a Negro mob scene, that is," she wrote in *Movin' on Up*. "The crowd was so big that Midtown traffic was all tied up. The box office sold out all the standing room and then put people up on the stage. When it was time for me to start singing, there was just a little place left for me next to the piano.

"I stood there gazing out at the thousands of men and women who had come to hear me, a baby nurse and washerwoman, on the stage where great artists like Enrico Caruso and Lily Pons and Marian Anderson had sung. I was afraid I wouldn't be able to make a sound. "Then I realized that all those colored people from Harlem and even from Baltimore and Boston were feeling a pride in themselves for my being up on that stage, for my being one of them. I began to sing with everything that was in me.

"The more I sang, the more the people in the audience clapped and cried out with joy. Some got up to dance in the aisles, with tears streaming down their faces. I got carried away, too, and found myself singing on my knees for them. I had to straighten up and say, 'Now we all must remember we're in Carnegie Hall, and if we cut up too much, they might put us out.'"

But nobody put her out. The white critics wrote "lovely" reviews, she discovered. After that, she gave a sold-out concert at Carnegie Hall nearly every year for the rest of her life.

Until 1950, she had dealt with white people relatively rarely. Her life in Chicago had been lived primarily in the Negro community, among her relatives and friends. When people came to visit her, she went into the kitchen and cooked southern specialties for them; sometimes they joined her and helped her cook the feasts. And on the road she had visited only the Negro communities. In Detroit, where she was often a guest of the Reverend Clarence L. Franklin, she went straight to his kitchen and began cooking collard greens. Her home-comings in New Orleans were always spent among her family and old friends, with meals as a center of attraction. Whites in her hometown knew nothing about her.

It's true that the owner of the Apollo label was a white woman, and Studs Terkel was white. But before she became involved in business and career meetings, most of her contacts with whites had taken place because she washed and pressed their laundry. Now suddenly she was catapulted to fame and fortune in the white world, and she was receiving more attention than ever in the African-American world, too. *Ebony* magazine published a story about gospel singers in December 1950, calling Mahalia and Sister Rosetta Tharpe the two best-known gospel singers in a field with many fine groups. Among them were the Pilgrim Travelers; J. Earle Hines; Sister Wynona Carr; the Ward Singers, founded by Gertrude Ward, mother of Clara Ward; and Robert Anderson; Brother Joe May; the Soul Stirrers; the Original Gospel Harmonettes; the Jubilee Singers; and the Jubilaires.

After she played at Carnegie Hall the first time, she discovered that the French had heard Hugues Panassie's broadcasts of her records and wanted her to go to France where they could hear her sing in person; they had given her France's venerable Charles Cros Academie Award. She was very flattered, but she hesitated at first, believing the Europeans couldn't possibly understand her songs.

So she continued traveling around the United States with her entourage, including an accompanist, James Francis, who was blind and who played the organ, and Mildred Falls, the pianist, and their driver. Harry Lenetska, too, went on some trips with the group. Mahalia had been appointed head of a Chicago church choir, but she had to give up that job because she was too busy touring. Pretty soon she had to sell her beauty salon; she didn't have time for that, either.

When she went back to Chicago, where she now lived on Michigan Avenue, her phone rang. It was Joe Bostic, saying that he had arranged for her to go to a meeting about jazz and its origins. Gospel singing had begun to develop in the mid-nineteenth century in black churches, and it was the immediate forerunner of the blues and jazz. Blues singers had taken the gospel rhythms and melodies and changed the words of the songs to tell stories about their daily, worldly lives. Jazz singers and musicians embellished blues and gospel melodies, harmonies, and rhythms. With each succeeding generation of jazz musicians, jazz became more sophisticated, encompassing the music of many cultures.

The meeting about jazz and its origins, Bostic told Mahalia, was going to be held at the Music Inn in Lenox, Massachusetts. Authorities in the classical music and jazz worlds were going to be there. Among them were John Mehegan, who would teach piano at the Juilliard School of Music and other colleges in New York; Richard Waterman of Northwestern University; Willis James of Spelman College; Marshall Stearns, a professor at Hunter College and a writer about jazz; and the famous jazz record producer John Hammond. Hammond had discovered a great jazz bandleader, Count Basie, and one of the legendary jazz singers, Billie Holiday. He had recorded them and blues singer Bessie Smith, clarinetist Benny Goodman, and many others for Columbia Records in the 1930s. None of the experts at the meeting in Lenox, Massachusetts—with the possible exception of John Hammond—had ever heard of Mahalia. She had certainly never heard of them. Bostic arranged for her to sing some gospel songs.

"I never expected to be singing for professors," Mahalia told Bostic. "But if they want me, I'll come, sure enough."

So she and Mildred Falls, Mahalia's musical soul sister, traveled to Lenox. There they found the Music Inn, once the carriage house on a former estate, where the symposium was being held. The estate was being remodeled for music lovers. When Mahalia and Mildred—both big, ample, bosomy women in early middle age—arrived, Mahalia found a busy scene. "Everybody was running around, carrying ladders and hammers, and people were sleeping in the stables and in the icehouse, which were being renovated." Mahalia knew that the place she was given to sleep in had been "an old horse stall," she said. She told Mildred, "I finally made it into the white folks' world and look where it landed me."

After supper, in a lounge in the main house, the professors asked Mahalia to get up on the stage and sing. She leaned against the piano and sang "Didn't It Rain!" and "Jesus Savior, Pilot Me," and "Movin' on Up." The words to the last song were, "One of these mornings I'm going to lay down my cross and get my crown; as soon as my feet strike Zion, I'm going to lay down my heavy burden; I'm going to put on my robes in glory and move on up a little higher."

She would reminisce later for her book, "As soon as I finished, a great big fuss busted loose. The professors started arguing with one another and asking me where I had learned to sing that way. Who had taught me? Where had I learned such tonal shading and rhythm?"

Mahalia actually never learned to read music, and when she was told to come in on a certain bar in a song, she asked to be told what word she was supposed to come in on. She sang from experience with audiences and by instinct about music and spiritual beliefs. "After they quieted down a little bit, I told them I'd been singing around Baptist churches and gospel tents and at prayer meetings all my life. I didn't learn to sing any special way. I just found myself doing it.

"Then they began carrying on all over again. They got out tape recorders and played some African bongo music and asked me if it sounded familiar. I told them I didn't know anything about jungle drums, but that the beat sounded good. It did something for me."

They asked Mahalia to sing again and again. When she woke up the next morning in the stable, she heard tape recordings of her songs and her own voice coming from the main house. She turned to Mildred Falls and said, "I mean to tell you right now, we're into something here with these crazy people, and I don't know what's going to happen next."

She and Mildred were kept at the conference for the whole week, while the experts asked her all kinds of questions about the music of the black churches, the blues, the field calls, and chants. The men kept trying to analyze her style. "Those professors were all mixed up," Mahalia would recall for *Newsweek* magazine on February 22, 1954. "They said I breathed right and made perfect tones. I just told them you're born with singing in you. Everything is right when singing comes from the soul." She didn't agree with the experts that her syncopated rhythms were African in origin. She thought her style came completely from her commitment to celebrating the Lord.

"Oh, they were nice to me. They were. But baby, here all these professors and Ph.D.'s picking at my music like birds at a box of corn, asking questions I didn't even understand what they were asking; I was so ashamed. And me got no more sense than to contend with those professors when they telling me what my music was made out of . . . but I *did* know what my foot was doing. It was tapping out four-four time and my singing come right out of the church, I did know that. Some of them getting excited about blues and jazz. I just flat-footed told them what I *knew*, and what I didn't know, no use trying to hide that. We ended up having us a time. We did."

John Hammond, who had left Columbia Records but would go back to the company by 1954, told her to think about recording for Columbia. She said she'd ponder his suggestion. Marshall Stearns, who was doing research for his brilliant history book *The Story of Jazz*, put Mahalia in the first pages: "She breaks every rule of concert singing, taking breaths in the middle of a word and sometimes garbling the words altogether, but the full-throated feeling and expression are seraphic," which meant that her voice sounded as if it came from the highest order of angels. Her singing at Lenox was so electrifying for the music authorities that Philip Barber told her, "Mahalia, if you'd started down to the lake while you were singing 'Shall We Gather at the River,' all those experts would have followed you right into the water to be baptized."

He didn't overstate their excitement about her singing. Mahalia was absolutely right when she sensed that something big was going to happen in her life. She went home to Chicago to find herself in the center of a gathering storm. "All those music professors must have gone home and talked to people in the church and concert field. Requests came pouring in. Ed Sullivan invited me to appear on his TV show," she would reminisce. Sullivan was the host of the most popular television variety show in the country at that time.

The French still wanted her to go to Paris and sing for them. She had thought it over and decided to go. If the French had been nice enough to give her an award, the least she could do was thank them in person. She would arrange a tour of Europe as soon as she took care of her growing number of prestigious and glamorous commitments in the United States, including another concert at Carnegie Hall in 1951 and her usual church-related performances. A Danish writer had already published an item in a periodical saying that Mahalia was interested in performing in Europe "but is a little scared. . . . This is something great for the concert halls. Mahalia would be a real attraction over here." However, she still felt most at ease performing in churches.

Mahalia Jackson's hometown of New Orleans, Louisiana,
at the turn of the century

Mahalia felt the Mardi Gras parade floats were beautiful but she always worried about the violent part of the annual celebration (above).

Singing at Mount Moriah Baptist Church as a child was the beginning of Mahalia's career. Gospel was her only musical choice (left).

Mahalia resisted jazz, though growing up in New Orleans she was familiar with the sounds of Louis Armstrong, shown here (lower center) with King Oliver's Band in 1923.

The metropolitan pace of Chicago was a big change for Mahalia when she moved there from Louisiana.

"All I do is add a little bounce," Mahalia said of her singing style (above).

When the Depression came, times were hard in Chicago. The men shown here are eating a hot meal provided by a Chicago soup kitchen (right).

Mahalia always put her heart into her music, as seen here during a recording session for Apollo Records in 1949. Mildred Falls, her longtime accompanist, is seen at the piano.

No matter what the occasion, Mahalia always spoke her mind (right).

Nat King Cole and Mahalia spent much time together during the filming of 1958's St. Louis Blues. She also appeared in the 1959 film Imitation of Life (below).

During her European tour in 1961, Mahalia sings a few notes for an attentive Munich porter (above).

Tommy Dorsey (on trombone) began as a Gospel musician, before turning his attention to jazz. He sometimes offered advice to Mahalia, but she never took it. She once told Duke Ellington (on piano) she'd never sing his kind of music, but he was inspired to write a suite for her called "Black, Brown and Beige."

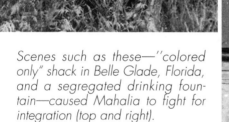

Scenes such as these—"colored only" shack in Belle Glade, Florida, and a segregated drinking fountain—caused Mahalia to fight for integration (top and right).

Mahalia became involved in the civil rights movement. She and Sammy Davis Jr. (with camera) both appeared on the program during the 1963 March on Washington.

In Anniston, Alabama, a racist group set fire
to this bus, carrying both black and white pasengers
who were demonstrating for integration in 1961.

In Jackson, Mississippi, African-Americans who dared to sit at a lunch counter were subjected to abuse from whites who poured ketchup, mustard, and sugar over their heads.

Dr. Martin Luther King Jr. won Mahalia's support and respect. He is seen here (waving to the crowd) with his wife and Dr. Ralph Bunche, leading a 1965 march for civil rights in Montgomery, Alabama.

Though her singing career was a great success, Mahalia's personal life often was difficult. Here she enjoys a moment of happiness with her second husband, Minters Galloway, at their wedding reception in July 1964.

Upon returning from her 1964 European tour, Mahalia sings a few bars aboard the SS United States (above).

During 1967, Mahalia was in great form singing on Easter Sunday at Philharmonic Hall in New York (right).

Mahalia sang with a natural energy, yet sometimes her health suffered. During her stay at Little Company of Mary Hospital, Chicago, in 1964, her spirits are uplifted by stacks of fan mail delivered by Sister Mary Luke. It was at this same hospital in 1972 that she would pass away.

Mahalia takes part in an impromptu rendition of "Just a Closer Walk with Thee" with the Eureka Brass Band at the 1970 New Orleans Jazz Festival (above).

Mahalia is in concert in 1969 (right). Earlier in her career, she was sometimes criticized for her exuberance, to which she replied, "Make a joyful noise unto the Lord, as David said."

More than 5,000 mourners attend Mahalia's funeral in 1972.

Aretha Franklin, who was inspired by Mahalia Jackson, sings "Precious Lord" at the funeral service for the Queen of Gospel.

MAHALIA'S WORLD WIDENS

In January 1951, Mahalia arrived with her entourage, including Joe Bostic, Harry Lenetska, who had arranged the date, John Sellers, and Mildred Falls, at the CBS studio on Broadway, from which Ed Sullivan broadcast his show, *Toast of the Town*, on Sunday nights. Mahalia saw other celebrities who would perform, but she didn't see an organ. She asked a man who looked as if he was in charge. He told her there was no provision for an organ for her. She asked where Mr. Sullivan was. When she was told he was in his dressing room, she headed there. Someone called after her that she couldn't disturb him. But she knocked and walked right in. Ed Sullivan was in his underwear.

"She was mad as hell," Sullivan later told Laurraine Goreau, laughing at the memory. He didn't want to give her the only organ in the studio, which was in his show's orchestra led by Ray Block. But that was what he ended up doing. Both Block and Sullivan were deeply moved by Mahalia's performance of the hymn "Dig a Little Deeper." Much to their delight, all the fan mail and audience response, even from the South, was favorable. "She was tremendous. . . . The audiences liked her instantly," Sullivan recalled. He was so in awe of her talent that he thought she should be an opera star. As for her personality, he said, "She was just so natural; she didn't give a damn whether they were black or white or yellow. She was just so darned kind to everybody. When Mahalia sang, she took command. . . . The woman was just great. The name that keeps coming to mind with me is Paul Robeson. He was the same type—and they didn't come into the theater with any inferiority complex. They knew that once the music started playing and they started singing, that was it. . . . She and I became very great friends. . . . For Mahalia, the single word I have is 'power.'"

From the CBS studio, Mahalia headed back to Chicago and went out on the gospel highway again, happy in the knowledge that Vogue Records, which distributed Apollo in Europe, was issuing her songs there. In Paris she would be awarded the 1951 Grand Prix du Disque—first prize—for her recordings. But life on the road was hectic. Some promoters were still trying to take more than their share of earnings from her performances. In Chicago the apartment house where she lived had a fire. Mahalia had to move into a hotel temporarily. By summertime Mildred Falls became ill, probably from exhaustion, and too weak to keep playing with Mahalia for a while. Mahalia planned to perform at Carnegie Hall again in October and head for Europe by the end of the year.

Then she too became ill. She started vomiting and gasping for breath as she traveled around the country in her car. When she sang in Atlanta, Georgia, about twenty-two thousand people showed up to hear her in a ballpark. But in the South her physical problems were compounded when she was refused service in some restaurants. When she returned to Chicago, she went to see a doctor. At first he suspected she was working too hard and eating too much. He advised her to diet and rest. But she kept working, and she didn't lose weight. By autumn, Mildred Falls was well again, but Mahalia was becoming sicker.

Through treatment and tests, doctors discovered she had growths in her uterus and needed a hysterectomy. Mahalia argued with the doctors: "I'm a gospel singer. I got to be on the boat for Europe in no time."

"You'll have a rough trip, if you go," said a doctor.

"Don't you worry 'bout Halie. I got strength in my mind," she said.

She didn't have the operation. On Columbus Day 1952, Mahalia performed for the third time at Carnegie Hall before three thousand people who paid four dollars a ticket. John Hammond wrote a review for *Down Beat*, one of the world's leading music magazines: "It took a very great artist to bring this music to the general public, and Mahalia Jackson is her name. Her power stems from a profound religious conviction, overwhelming rhythmic vitality, and a voice capable of projecting every emotion. If the vocal cords can withstand the tremendous strain to which they are subjected, Mahalia will be the most successful folksinger of our time."

She sang only four songs because she had the flu. Joe Bostic explained to the audience that Mahalia was ill. People cheered for her anyway. Others on the bill that night were the Ward Singers with Clara Ward, whose recordings for Savoy and Gotham rivaled Mahalia's for popularity; the Davis Sisters from Philadelphia; and Norsalus McKissick, a member of the gospel group the Gospelaires, who won special praise from Hammond.

A few days later, on October 17, Mahalia, looking gray and exhausted, boarded the S.S. *United States* and sailed for Le Havre, France. Arriving just as tired as she had been when she left home, she headed for the Salle Pleyel in Paris to give a concert. There she met Hugues Panassie and embraced and kissed him. Immediately they liked each other. Then it was time for her to go onstage.

She was in pain, burning up with fever, and short of breath. With her was Harry Lenetska. Frightened by her physical problems, Mahalia said, "Harry, read me the Twenty-Seventh psalm." He did: "The Lord is my light and my salvation; whom shall I fear? The Lord is the strength of my life; of whom shall I be afraid?" Mahalia miraculously felt well again, so strong-willed was she. She went onstage, delivered an inspired performance, and came offstage drained of energy. The next night the same thing happened. But she wouldn't give up the tour. More than twenty thousand people heard her in four days in Paris. Newspaper and magazine stories sent back to the United States said audiences wept while she sang, though they didn't understand her lyrics. Police were called in to keep mobs of teenagers from swarming over her.

When she sang in Lyons and Bordeaux, she became weak after each performance. But she kept going. Mahalia loved French audiences; they clapped on the right beat—the offbeat. But she was very tired, she told her friends and the French critics whom she had just met. She was losing weight.

In London, at Royal Albert Hall, which was cold that winter, she struggled to her feet, took a deep breath, and went onstage. Winston Churchill and the queen of England sent greetings to her. One critic wrote about "the soaring beauty and extraordinary tone." Another said that "her voice combines the simplicity and warmth of classic folksingers like Bessie [Smith, and] . . . the artistry, power and distinction of concert stars like Marian Anderson." But offstage, unseen by the audience, Mahalia collapsed.

She struggled to her feet and went to sing on the British Broadcasting Corporation. Among the people who waited for her to come out of the studio and sign autographs were young members of a jazz band. They asked if she would be president of their band. "Oh, those children were wonderful all over Europe. Everywhere I went, they were there," she would reminisce for a Down Beat magazine writer two years later. Similar attention was paid to her at Southampton, Oxford, and Birmingham, England, and in Copenhagen, Denmark, where her two performances were sold out.

She sang "Silent Night" on a Danish radio broadcast, and people called the station to order the record. Some reports said two thousand orders came in; others said twenty thousand, which Mahalia thought was the correct figure. Denmark presented her with a Castle Kronenberg vase usually reserved for royalty, according to a writer for CBS. Children brought flowers to her hotel and strewed them on the steps.

She struggled through Rome, southern Italy, and Morocco, until Lenetska reasoned with her. It was a hysterectomy that she needed, and then she could go on with the world tour. She had hoped to go on to the Holy Land, to see Jerusalem at last and to sing there, before her tour ended. But she had lost ninety pounds; her pulse was erratic. She went back to Paris, where she fainted onstage. Doctors examined her and told her that she shouldn't travel. Even so, she made arrangements to fly back to Chicago, because she didn't want to be operated on in Europe.

In late November, still fearful of the operation, Mahalia asked for a reading of the Twenty-seventh Psalm as she was being taken into surgery and given an anesthetic. When she woke up, she felt much better. The growths in her uterus had been large, and they were gone. By mid-December she was out of the hospital, with orders to eat lean food. She was buoyed up, too, by her memories of the respectful way white people had treated her in Europe. And she went home to a houseful of people ready to take care of her. Among them was Little Brother John Sellers, who rubbed her feet. She told him she regarded him as a son. By January, she had recovered and was back on the gospel highway, touring the country.

For her stay in New York in October 1953, when she gave her next concert at Carnegie Hall, she moved into the Wellington Hotel. That was the first time she had stayed in a white hotel in Midtown. New York hotels had not opened their doors to African-Americans until this time; Mahalia had previously stayed in Harlem hotels and traveled downtown to work. Many famous African-American entertainers, Nat King Cole among them, had done the same thing for years. In 1953, too, the new talent chief of Columbia Records, Mitch Miller, went to Carnegie Hall to hear her sing. John Hammond had been telling him that Columbia must have Mahalia as one of the recording artists.

Miller was surprised when Mahalia didn't jump at his offer of a contract for fifty thousand dollars. She called John

Hammond for advice. He told her Columbia would promote her and advertise her records, but she might lose touch with her own people; Columbia knew nothing about gospel music. Mahalia had lunch with Mitch Miller, who suggested she sing the blues, and Mahalia explained she sang only the gospel. He still wanted her to sign the contract. She was unable to make up her mind.

She was very familiar with Bess Berman's Apollo label, and she could renew her contract with that company. But she also believed that Bess's company had shortchanged her. Mahalia pondered the situation as she traveled around the country singing and eating—and praying for the Lord's guidance about what to do. Finally she decided to take a chance with Columbia. As soon as she did that, she was offered a CBS network radio show, half an hour long, to be broadcast from Chicago. The *New York Daily Mirror* columnist Sidney Fields, in his column "Only Human," on October 14, 1954, wrote that Miller had told radio and television producer Louis Cowan about Mahalia. Cowan rushed to Chicago to make a record of her singing on a Monday and sent it to CBS president William S. Paley. By Friday she had her own radio show, to be broadcast on WBBM from Chicago on Sunday nights between 10:05 P.M. and 10:30 P.M. Eastern Standard Time, beginning in October 1954. "That's what you call the power of prayer," Mahalia told Sidney Fields. "I prayed hard before that record was made."

She insisted on hiring Studs Terkel as her writer, even though he was running into political difficulties because of his leftist-leaning, liberal outlook on social issues. Senator Joseph McCarthy, who was on a witch-hunt for Communists, took a dim view of Terkel and wanted to brand him a Communist. McCarthy attacked many people unfairly. They lost their jobs in the 1950s. But Mahalia insisted on having her way. She hired Terkel, and nobody bothered her. Before she started making records for Columbia, her show made her voice more familiar to audiences all around the country. She had truly moved up.

By 1954, she was earning fifty thousand dollars a year gross, said several writers, but *Life* magazine estimated her income at one hundred thousand dollars gross. That was more likely—and possibly an understatement. Her CBS recording contract alone was for fifty thousand; she was doing a radio show, performing in churches, and collecting royalties from fifty records she had made for Apollo, several of them estimated to have sold a million copies.

But she had gained too much weight, her doctor told her. She was back up to 220 pounds, putting a strain on her health.

7

QUEEN OF THE GOSPEL ONSTAGE, EMBATTLED AFRICAN-AMERICAN OFFSTAGE

Mahalia's effervescent personality made her well loved by audiences and by everyone connected with her shows. She taped them before they were broadcast. For one thing, she could not be in Chicago every Sunday to do a live broadcast. And sometimes her shows ran for more than thirty minutes. They could have been cut off the air. It was better for her to tape shows and have them edited. Her studio audiences cheered for her singing and helped give her shows special warmth. One critic wrote: "When Mahalia begins to sing, even the elevator men in the building begin to bounce. The audience wept with 'Summertime,' rocked with 'Joshua Fit the Battle of Jericho' and was so fractured by 'Didn't It Rain!' that they had to call intermission." Once, when an audience began stamping, Mahalia warned them, "Don't you start that or we'll tear this studio apart. You got to remember, we're not in church—we're on CBS." She had refused to let her shows be taped during church services, saying that she didn't want to embarrass people who might be carried away by the excitement and put on an exuberant show of their faith. She remained protective of the spiritual roots of her singing.

Her show brought gospel music to many white people for the first time. A beautiful actress, Faye Emerson, who had become a broadcast personality herself, wrote an article for the *New York World–Telegram and Sun*, on September 25, 1954, just before the debut of the show *Mahalia*, saying that she had heard of Mahalia only recently. A guest on Faye Emerson's radio show, Marshall Stearns, had introduced Faye to Mahalia's record of "Silent Night," done for Apollo. "It had a strange but fascinating sound. This Negro uses her voice much as a jazz musician improvises with his instrument. . . . Mahalia Jackson has a deep spiritual quality that makes this . . . very moving." Obviously some white people were having culture shock and loving it.

At the urging of her show's Irish sponsor and Jewish producer, she learned Irish and Jewish songs. She liked the plaintive tone of the Jewish songs, and she became known for singing the haunting "Danny Boy." "I got to love both kinds [of songs]," she said in her book, *Movin' on Up*. They seemed religious and spiritual to her, and they didn't take anything away from her pledge to sing only gospel music. After six months she began doing a local television show on Sunday nights in Chicago. "People wrote in about how much they liked the program, so that I got carried away and one day at a meeting at the television station I said, 'Why don't we make this a network show instead of a local Chicago program? Then I can sing to a lot more people.'"

She noticed that everyone seemed embarrassed. One of the men spoke up: "We'd love to, Mahalia, but we can't do it. You're all right here in Chicago with a local sponsor, but there isn't a sponsor who sells his product down south that would take a chance on a Negro singer. They're afraid the southerners wouldn't like it."

Mahalia never got a national television show. Jules Schwerin said in his book that her stint on radio lasted only twenty weeks and the half hour was cut down to ten minutes for the last three shows because she couldn't get a sponsor. Also, the television show she starred in wasn't actually her own; it was a WBBM-TV show called *In Town Tonight*, featuring various Chicago-based celebrities. But the reason behind all versions of her dilemma was the same: as an African-American, she couldn't attract a sponsor.

It wasn't until the next year, 1956, that NBC tried to launch an African-American star, Nat King Cole, in a network television show. In the 1990s, when African-American television stars can't satisfy all the calls by sponsors, it is difficult to imagine Cole once had to use a variety of sponsors in different regions of the country. Advertising agencies said they couldn't find major national advertisers for him. Sponsors were afraid of reaction in the South. NBC paid about twenty thousand dollars a week to sustain Cole's show for a year. Mahalia was always welcomed as a guest on shows with white hosts eager to have her; among them were Steve Allen, Ed Sullivan, Bing Crosby, and Dinah Shore. She made a big hit singing a duet with Dinah. White southerners and northerners, easterners and westerners always wrote to her about how much they loved her singing. Cole came to think that the advertising agencies on Madison Avenue "were afraid of the dark," he said. He predicted that one day all the advertising problems for African-American stars would end, and he was correct.

Mahalia would later write in her autobiography that she was frustrated by the racial mess in the country: "It's just that when you move back and forth between the white and colored worlds every day, the stupidity and cruelty of some white people toward the Negro hits you so hard you don't know whether to explode or pray for someone who has such hatred in his soul." When she stepped off the stage, some white people were still likely to treat her as if she had leprosy, she said.

In the mid-1950s, she wanted to buy her own house in Chicago. While she was driving around town, she saw a lovely house with a For Sale sign in a white neighborhood. The owner was a white surgeon who said he would be proud to sell it to her. Mahalia paid forty thousand dollars for the house. "Well, when the news got around his neighborhood, the people almost went crazy," she recalled for Movin' on Up, and for interviewers. "Everybody was holding meetings up and down the block. You'd have thought the atomic bomb was coming instead of me." Some people used the telephone to threaten that, if she moved in, they would blow up the red-brick, ranch-style house with dynamite. "You're going to need more than your gospel songs to save you," said a warning voice.

"They got me so upset that I prayed to God every night to guide me in the right thing to do. I hadn't intended to start a one-man crusade. All I wanted was a quiet, pretty house to live in. Finally I bought this house," she said.

Someone fired a shotgun pellet through a window. Police were posted outside for almost a year. She credited Democratic mayor Richard Daley with helping to keep her safe. He would become a controversial figure for his tough, conservative politics in the future, but he always had Mahalia's support. Edward R. Murrow, host of the CBS show *Person to Person*, quickly asked her to broadcast as his guest from her house. When Murrow's crew moved all of their cameras and telephone and lighting equipment to her street, about three thousand people gathered to watch. A few people came to the door and asked if they could help her. She told them she would love to have them round up all the children they could find to appear on her show.

"Their mothers dressed them up, white and colored," she recalled, "and they all came, and we had a wonderful time. I cooked up a Louisiana Everything Gumbo, red beans . . . rice. We all ate, cameramen, children, neighbors, everybody." Some of her neighbors began to sell their houses, but the opposition to her living in the neighborhood died down. Murrow's show had helped a great deal.

Despite the turmoil she faced there, she preferred to live in Chicago rather than in the South. In Chicago she felt free. Each time she visited New Orleans, the rigid segregation felt like a slap in the face. She would not be served at a soda fountain in New Orleans until 1962. Jules Schwerin, who heard her sing at an outdoor gospel meeting in New York State and wanted to do a film about her, ended up writing his book, *Got to Tell It*, instead. He visited her in New Orleans on one of her trips home. He flew ahead from New York. She drove her lavender-colored Cadillac down from Chicago. She needed a big car to carry her group to her singing engagements, and the color was her taste.

Schwerin was worried when she didn't arrive on the appointed day, but her half-brother, Johnny Jackson, didn't think the delay was odd. When she did arrive, she called Schwerin at his hotel and invited him to join her at her brother's little cabin on Water Street. There she told Schwerin that she had been late because of an "abusive racial confrontation with the Louisiana State Police." She had been driving through the countryside when a police siren pierced the quiet night air. Two troopers stopped her and asked her angrily whose car she was driving. They called her "bitch" and seemed not to recognize her. She was glad, because she thought they might suspect she was carrying a large amount of money and take it from her. Mahalia told them the car belonged to her "madam." "She don't drive, she even makes me have the registration in my own name," Mahalia said. Schwerin recounted the story in his book.

The police told her to take off her shoes so they could make sure she had no money hidden there. They demanded to know if she had a money belt, but they didn't pursue that line of questioning. They forced her to empty her pocketbook, and in her stuffed wallet, they found five hundred dollars. Then they ordered her to go with them to a town marshal's office, where they lied, telling the marshal that she had been speeding. She was fined two hundred fifty dollars. The troopers handed her back fifty dollars. She didn't see which one took the two hundred dollars for himself. They watched her drive off, without any idea how relieved she was that they hadn't searched her clothes and found the rest of her money, which she had tucked into her underwear. She often carried thousands of dollars that way.

In New Orleans, she was cordial and kind to Schwerin, taking him around town in her striking Cadillac. She introduced him to friends who welcomed him because he was with her, but she made him ride in the backseat because, she said, that was required by the city's segregation laws. Schwerin didn't know if that seating arrangement was actually a law, but he did as he was directed. Her friends shook her hand or embraced her and smiled at him and shook his hand. Her brother told Schwerin that he was the third white man ever to come into his house. The other two were a policeman and a tax collector. Schwerin had the feeling that a storm was coming in race relations in the South.

Nearly thirty years later, a prominent New Orleans blues and jazz guitarist and banjo player, Danny Barker, required that a visiting northern journalist sit in the backseat of his car while he drove her around. He took her to an integrated musical event he played for, told her what she wanted to know about early jazz music, and pointed to former slave quarters still standing behind a mansion. The segregation laws had changed by then, but Barker still preferred to go along with old customs. In 1955 Mahalia had told Schwerin that if a policeman came to check her license, or if the car wasn't operating properly, and Schwerin wasn't sitting in the backseat, she would just jump out of the car and run and leave it to him.

Though conditions were far from perfect for her in Chicago, she never wanted to move back to New Orleans. She welcomed writers of all races, many of them avid new fans, to the places where she lived. In the 1950s she lived for a while in a five-room apartment on Chicago's South Side before moving to her house. She had lavish, bright-looking furnishings. In the house she had French provincial furniture and gold and plush upholstery, one writer reported. Another mentioned the photographs she kept of the great contralto Marian Anderson, the basso Paul Robeson, both known to be among her favorite singers, and even Liberace, the pop singer and pianist, whom she liked for his appealing sweetness. Everybody was welcome at her dining table, where her family, friends, and even such celebrities as Duke Ellington came to dine. One writer recalled that Duke Ellington played jazz on the piano after dinner one night, and Mahalia had told him she could never sing what he was playing.

In the 1950s, Duke wrote a suite for her called *Black, Brown and Beige.* It was part of a body of his work that he called his sacred music. He told her she had inspired him to compose it. She would eventually make a portion of it, called "Come Sunday," a classic on a recording and at a Newport Jazz Festival in 1958.

Visitors always spoke of the crowd of people cooking all the time in Mahalia's kitchen. Among the many writers who would describe Mahalia's hospitality was Carlton Brown, who published an article in *Harper's* magazine in August 1956. By that time, her first three Columbia albums had been issued. Carlton, interviewing her on a tape recorder, later claimed that his machine "picked up the sizzle of frying onions and okra in the background."

"I come up with this recipe," said Mahalia. "Of course, the way we cook it down home in New Orleans, everything is fresh." She went on to explain the way they grew vegetables and fished in the Mississippi. "People seem to think it's a little odd for a singer like me to do her own cooking and housework, like I do, but this is the real part of me. I was doing this long before I ever thought I'd be a singer."

Carlton was charmed by her serene expression and satin-smooth complexion. He thought she looked far younger than her forty-five years. Mahalia explained that gospel music was almost two thousand years old. "When Christ was born, people went forth and sang in joy. That was gospel music. Joy and the spreading of good tidings. That is what it still is." Carlton asked her why she had called blues songs "sinful" and turned down engagements in nightclubs and theaters that would have paid her ten thousand dollars a week.

"There's no sense in my singing the blues, because I just don't feel it," she said. "In the old, heartfelt songs, whether it's the blues or gospel music, there's the distressed cry of a human being. But in the blues, it's all despair; when you're done singing, you're still lonely and sorrowful. In the gospel songs, there's mourning and sorrow, too, but there's always hope and consolation to lift you above it. I must sing a song that is an uplift to myself and can help lift the burden of others. If I sing, 'Nobody knows the trouble I've seen, nobody knows but Jesus,' there's sorrow in it, but there is the uplift and redemption of his love. He knows the trouble I see, and he alone will lift me above my troubles. It's not that you're lifted out of segregation or poverty or sickness, but it lifts your mind above, that you can endure those things. It gives hope that whatever may abide, whatever is wrong in the neighborhood or the world, tomorrow will be better.

"I have many fine friends who entertain in nightclubs and theaters, but it's not the place for my kind of singing. They got enough out there. I don't think that people dancing and having a nice time and going to the theater's a sin. What I think is a sin is going against the commandment to love the Lord thy God with all your heart and love thy neighbor as thyself. You cannot serve God unless you love each other. A person that's religious doesn't have to be a punk or a sissy because he loves the Lord; he loves Him because He loves you and *[me]*."

Carlton's article also spoke of Mahalia's joyfulness about her success. She had kept singing throughout the years of poverty because she loved to sing: "I sing because I'm happy, I sing because I'm free," as she often affirmed in her hymn "His Eye Is on the Sparrow." She had never expected riches to come from her gospel singing. But when they did, they were an added reason to sing with an overflowing spirit.

One time she left New York City, where she had sung to sold-out houses, and traveled to perform in Nashville, Tennessee. She was carrying her money in a little white suitcase. And the white suitcase reminded her of her mother in a little white coffin on a skiff being carried across the river for burial. She told one of the women traveling with her, "That suitcase carries me back to my childhood." She spoke about her mother's death and her own childhood full of hard labor. "Coming up, I never had a Christmas tree. I never had a doll. But look at that suitcase. God has given me enough money to buy me a doll."

As she stood arranging her hair with a curling iron, she started to sing. Her friend recalled, "Ooooh, my God! Listen! That woman sing so till the streetcar stopped in front of the hotel and all the people just come out of the streetcar and they were standing looking all in the windows. . . . We couldn't stop her. She stood there for two hours, and every time we tried to stop her, she said, 'But God gave me enough money to buy me a doll.' Oh, Jesus! My God! The people were shouting all out in the street—screaming—everywhere! We couldn't even dress her. You couldn't do anything with her. For two hours." Whenever her friend tried to stop her, Mahalia said again, "God gave me enough money to buy me a doll!"

Her friend also said that Mahalia hadn't changed a bit because of her fame. People still called out to her, "Hey, Halie," on the street. And once, when she was singing "A City Called Heaven," on television, she was so carried away by the music that she closed her eyes and began to cry. "Tears came a-streaming down her cheeks," her friend said, "and before she knew it she had cried out, 'O Glory!' on the air. Then she said, 'Pardon me, CBS—forgot where I was.'" Calls came in to the station from everywhere, said her friend.

Calls for public service came to her, too. In the 1950s she began singing the gospel at the invitation of ministers who wanted her voice to lift the spirits of the people who were fighting for equal rights.

8

MAHALIA LINKS HER CAREER TO THE CIVIL RIGHTS MOVEMENT AND NATIONAL POLITICS

In the mid-1950s, Mahalia began singing for the civil rights movement. The 1950s were a time of growing ferment. The laws of the land were changing. First came the school desegregation act in 1954. Equal opportunity acts would come in the 1960s. When she went to Denver, Colorado, to sing at a Baptist convention, a minister introduced her to two young Southern Baptist ministers, the Reverend Ralph D. Abernathy, who was pastor of a church in Montgomery, Alabama, and a young divinity school graduate. He was pastor of the Dexter Avenue Baptist Church, an old church in Montgomery, and his name was Reverend Martin Luther King Jr. Mahalia had known his parents for many years. His father was pastor of the Ebenezer Baptist Church in Atlanta, Georgia, and his grandfather had been a pastor there, too.

In 1954, in the South, the school desegregation act had stirred up whites and African-Americans. Then, just before Christmas in 1955, a woman named Rosa Parks, who worked as a seamstress, refused to go to the back of a bus to sit down. Segregation dictated that African-Americans must ride in the back seats of the public buses. Mrs. Parks simply decided not to do it. She was arrested, and she went down in the history books as the person who lit a match that set the southern segregation laws aflame. It would be years before the fire went out. But the papers on which the segregation laws were written would turn to ashes.

The Reverend Martin Luther King Jr., was leading people in support of Mrs. Parks. She was brought to trial for her refusal to move to the back of a bus. One day, about half of the fifty thousand African-Americans in Montgomery refused to ride the city buses to protest her trial. The next day about 90 percent joined the boycott of the buses. Reverend King and Reverend Abernathy had organized the Montgomery Improvement Association to raise money for car pools to transport African-Americans to and from their jobs. At the convention in Denver, Reverend Abernathy asked Mahalia if she would go to Montgomery and sing at a rally to raise money for the cause. She said she would be pleased to go. He asked her how much she would charge. Mahalia told him, "Man, I ain't coming to Montgomery to make no money off them walking folks."

She stayed at the Abernathy house, ate the southern food she loved with the family, and went to Saint John African Methodist Episcopal church, the biggest African-American church in the city. People drifted to the church all afternoon for the eight o'clock service. Mahalia saw police everyplace and some white men who she believed were troublemakers, but the service proceeded peacefully. With her eyes closed, she sang "I've Heard of a City Called Heaven." The applause was thunderous. Ted Poston, a reporter for the *New York Post*, wrote an article published on December 7, 1956: "The rafters rang with 'Sing the song, girl,' and 'Oh, yes, God, oh, yes, Jesus,' from the congregation. One aging celebrant suddenly leaped to her feet, bowling over several participants. Three sisters quietly restrained her, and Mahalia subdued the tumult with a soft rendition of 'Silent Night, Holy Night.'"

She thought the service was a great success. But a few days after she left town a bomb exploded in the Abernathy house and destroyed the living room and a bedroom.

Churches and houses owned by other African-Americans and white sympathizers were blown up, too. Women were fired from their jobs. Men were told to get out of town. But the African-Americans, led by King and Abernathy, didn't abandon the boycott. They kept walking all winter and right through the next summer rather than ride the segregated buses. The bus lines tried to fight the boycott by raising their fares, but they were desperate for customers. The U.S. Supreme Court finally handed down its verdict: segregation in the buses was unconstitutional.

Mahalia was happy that the tactic of nonviolent resistance, which King and Abernathy preached, was victorious. She became close friends with Dr. King. She brought him to her house and cooked him sumptuous southern meals when he came to talk in Chicago and raise funds for the cause.

He moved to Atlanta and became a minister at his father's church, where he founded the Southern Christian Leadership Conference. That organization was committed to fighting in nonviolent ways for equal rights. Some whites formed White Citizens Councils to try to counteract the movement. The struggle was on full blast. Mahalia applauded the formation of all types of groups by young African-Americans, some of them students—the Students' Central Committee founded in Nashville, and the Student Non-Violent Coordinating Committee in Atlanta. She knew that some northerners, both African-American and white, joined the groups, too, but mostly southerners spearheaded the groups. Some were controversial; their leaders said and did inflammatory things that worried whites who wanted to see equal rights brought about slowly and quietly by legal means. But the laws weren't working. The youngsters pushed for better laws and momentous, quick changes in society right away. Throughout the late 1950s Mahalia stayed busy consolidating her reputation as the Queen of the Gospel Singers. She steadfastly refused to sing anything but the gospel or songs that she felt implied the uplift of religion or a God-oriented spirituality. "You'll Never Walk Alone" and "I Believe" were among them. She never sang in a jazz club. She would even have refused to sing with the Duke

Ellington jazz orchestra, except that she respected the sacred music Duke had written especially for her.

John S. Wilson, the dean of jazz critics, who wrote for *The New York Times*, said about Mahalia singing Duke's "Come Sunday," "She was an apt choice, for she [sent] this haunting Ellington melody soaring with her fervent and, in this case, carefully disciplined projection." She also sang with jazz musicians in her groups in Columbia's studios. For that, she came under some criticism from churchpeople. It was true that jazz groups accompanying her sometimes made the music sound more commercial and less churchy than her performances with Mildred Falls on piano and an organ accompanist. Churchpeople thought she was using the jazzier sound of true jazz musicians to appeal to white audiences who might not sufficiently appreciate and buy her orthodox gospel work. For one of her early recordings for Columbia, in November 1954, she sang "Walk over God's Heaven," with the white guitarist Art Ryerson adding his commercially piquant and sunny embellishments. She herself thought her work was usually best when accompanied only by piano and organ, with players who came from the Baptist church background, such as Mildred Falls and the organist Ralph Jones. But Mahalia's recordings with Duke Ellington were exquisite. Though she refused to sing in jazz clubs, she accepted invitations to sing at the Newport Jazz Festival in Rhode Island.

Reviews for her work at Newport in 1957 were so good that it seemed they could never be topped. However, the concert she gave there in 1958 was even better, one of the great ones of her career. At the peak of her powers, she was recorded live in concert at Newport by Columbia. An independently produced movie called *Jazz on a Summer's Day* also captured the spirit of the event. It quickly became a classic shown in movie theaters all around the world. When videos became a popular form of home entertainment, *Jazz on a Summer's Day* became available to an even wider public.

First she performed "Come Sunday" and a gospel song with Duke Ellington's orchestra in a jazz concert at Newport. She had already performed the song with him in a studio for a Columbia recording the previous year. That was the first time she had ever sung with an orchestra, and she didn't know how to do it. "And Duke Ellington is a man that don't rehearse nothing!" she would reminisce for the noted jazz critic Ralph J. Gleason for an article in the *New York Journal American* on September 26, 1959. "He hits the piano and says: 'Sing!' and I says, 'Sing what?' and that's how we made [the album] *Black, Brown and Beige!* That man! I'm telling you! Him being so great! I was afraid to act like I didn't know. But after I got through, I felt very proud. When we did 'The Lord's Prayer,' there I had my Bible."

Her own concert at Newport took place early on a Sunday morning. She sang "The Lord's Prayer" with the creamiest of voices, reminiscent of the legendary jazz singer Sarah Vaughan's. And her heavenly vibrato and rapturous embellishments helped create the glorious sound of her total conviction. Anyone listening to her was "told," as gospel singers say. And only if you listen to her will you know what it means to be told, and to be glad you were told—"so glad, so glad," as Mahalia frequently added to her hymns and spirituals. When she sang "mmmmm" instead of words, she implied the wordless spirit.

No more exciting version of the pop spiritual "Didn't It Rain!" exists than her version at the Newport concert: "Talk about rain all night, Oh, my Lord, oh, didn't it rain, rain forty days, forty nights, without stopping. Knock on the window, knock on the door, Brother Noah, can't you take on more . . . full of sin. . . . God got the key, can't get in." Her audience roared. Some people that rainy morning claimed that, once she sang that song, the rain stopped. She could sing anything, and no matter how simple or unimportant it was in the hierarchy of the gospel literature, she made it transcendent. She gave the deceptively simple "I'm on My Way," with its repeated lyric, her full, swinging, bouncy, percussive, soulful treatment. Nobody could clap with more authority than Mahalia.

Finally she arrived at a place in her concert where she could start her encores. "Now I don't know if you want to hear me and want to stay in the rain. I'm just getting warmed up. All right, you make me feel like I'm a star," said the most famous gospel singer in the world in her sweet, natural way— the singer whose voice came "once in a millennium," as Reverend Martin Luther King Jr. described it. On she went with "Joshua Fit the Battle of Jericho" and "Jesus Met the Woman at the Well," with Mildred Falls playing piano as if she shared Mahalia's spirit. Mildred knew exactly when to play prettily, percussively, jubilantly, or with bluesy feeling or a decorative trill. After Mahalia sang "The Lord's Prayer," Mildred knew that she should solo for a long time to allow the audience to recover and get ready for Mahalia's shout, "I'm going to walk all over God's heaven, heaven, oh, yes, heaven"—Mahalia's grittiest, growling-est song that night. Some critics called the concert "miraculous."

Bass player Milt Hinton, a jazz musician, was hired to do a great deal of work in the recording studios in these years. Like Mahalia, he had been brought up in a Southern Baptist church and had moved to Chicago as a child. He frequently recorded with Mahalia, working on an album of Christmas music that included her beloved and venerated "Silent Night." He understood her and loved working with her. She didn't like fooling around much in the studio. Mildred first told the musicians the keys and the number of choruses that Mahalia wanted for her songs. "Then Mahalia came in and just got right with it," Hinton recalled. "She wanted us to swing, but she didn't want us stomping too much. And she and Mildred were swinging." Hinton especially admired Mildred's ability to play the piano. "And Mahalia was a friendly, dear lady and very religious," he would always recall.

She gave countless concerts in auditoriums such as New York's Town Hall, where she shared top place with the French baritone of the Metropolitan Opera, Martial Singher, and performances in Philharmonic Hall in New York, in churches in Chicago and other major cities, and in little towns, too. She even appeared in movies, first *St. Louis Blues* starring Nat King

Cole in the role of blues composer W. C. Handy, though she never went to see it in a theater. The reviews were not very good for the movie anyway. She would later play herself, singing one gospel song in the 1959 movie *Imitation of Life*, which fared slightly better with the critics. She set up the Mahalia Jackson Foundation and gave small grants to young gospel singers to help them through the early days of trial and error in their careers. One of the grants was for one hundred dollars, a tidy sum for a young singer to receive in those days. If Mahalia had been able to get that herself when she was struggling financially, it would have been a windfall beyond her wildest dreams.

At the end of the 1950s, *Ebony* magazine estimated that her gross income was as high as one million dollars a year. Most other sources said her total income was one hundred thousand dollars a year, but that figure seems low. It's possible that nobody really knew how much she earned. Mahalia accepted many of her fees in cash. The most accurate accounting of her earnings was probably kept by Mahalia in her head. She never stopped singing in churches, though her wealth came primarily from concerts and records, and she had sung for Presidents Truman and Eisenhower by then. She was chosen to sing for Eisenhower during his three-day birthday celebration in Abilene, Kansas, in 1959.

Though she was mightily impressed and grateful for her celebrity, she was constantly reminding people that her career belonged to the church. Over the next few years she would say repeatedly that it was the message, not the money, that counted. She never seemed to have the slightest attachment to show business except as a practical concern. When she wasn't emphasizing the gospel for itself, she was fascinated by the politics and progress of the civil rights movement.

In Greensboro, North Carolina, in 1960, the young people she admired walked into drugstores and five-and-ten-cent stores, sat down, and waited to be served. And the movement spread to lunch counters and libraries all over the South. That was the era of sit-ins, when the protesters refused to answer back or hit back if they were attacked verbally or physically. Their leaders instructed them to turn the other cheek and hold their ground. Over a period of two years, the youngsters eradicted segregation with their sit-ins at movie houses, lunch counters, and other public facilities in many southern states—North Carolina, South Carolina, Tennessee, and Virginia.

Reverend Martin Luther King Jr. took part in the sit-ins in Georgia. In October 1960 he was sentenced to four months at hard labor in the Georgia State Penitentiary, where he could have been killed. President Eisenhower did nothing. But John F. Kennedy, who was running for president, put his brother Robert F. Kennedy to work on the case. Robert spoke to the judge who had sentenced King, and the next day King was free. Word of the Kennedy brothers' actions spread through African-American communities. Reverend King Sr., who had been wary of the Catholic Church, threw his support to the Kennedys. The African-American vote was crucial to the Kennedy victory in some states in November 1960.

After the election, Mahalia received a phone call from actor Peter Lawford, who was married to Patricia Kennedy, the president's sister. Would Mahalia go to the inauguration and sing "The Star-Spangled Banner"? She immediately accepted and started practicing the national anthem in her kitchen while she cooked. She had never sung it in public. The week of the inauguration she set off by train with Mildred Falls, a Democratic congressman who had been her friend for years, Mayor Daley, and the publisher of *Ebony* magazine.

Singer Frank Sinatra, a friend of Peter Lawford's and, in those days, of the Kennedys, too, had gotten some of the most celebrated people in the entertainment world to go to the inauguration. Mahalia saw comedians Milton Berle, Jimmy Durante, and Joey Bishop and singers Nat King Cole, Harry Belafonte, Ella Fitzgerald, and others. Bette Davis and Fredric March were there. In New York City a few hit shows were closed down so that Sir Laurence Olivier, Anthony Quinn, and Ethel Merman could go to Washington for the celebration. Leonard Bernstein conducted the orchestra. Actor Sidney Poitier and dancer Gene Kelly arrived. Actors Tony Curtis and Janet

Leigh, who were then married, joined an audience of about twelve thousand people. People had warned Mahalia about Frank Sinatra's temper, but he greeted her with a kiss on the cheek; she stopped being nervous. The glamour of the occasion astounded her.

Rehearsals went smoothly. But for the main event, nothing went right. A storm piled up so much snow in the streets that nobody could get to the gala on time. Mahalia and Mildred barely made it to the armory, and automobiles, buses, and streetcars were having trouble getting through the snowdrifts. About an hour and a half after the show was supposed to start, Leonard Bernstein and a seventy-piece orchestra played "The Stars and Stripes Forever," then "Anchors Aweigh" in honor of President Kennedy, who had been a naval hero during World War II.

After all the celebrities were marched in from the side entrances to their seats, Mahalia stood up. The theater lights dimmed. And she sang "The Star-Spangled Banner." The rest of the show went on until almost two o'clock in the morning. It was followed by a party. There Mahalia met Vice President Lyndon Baines Johnson, whose family she thought was very sweet. Johnson would eventually shepherd important civil rights legislation through Congress. "It was a lovely party that looked as beautiful to me as a biblical revelation," she said in *Movin' on Up.*

At 3:00 A.M., President Kennedy, whom she had never met before—"a tall young man in a blue suit," she saw—came to her table to say he had loved her singing for a long time and was thankful she had come to open the gala for him. "He looked into my eyes as if he was looking right into my soul, and I suddenly knew how he was able to draw people to him in a magnetic way. He made me feel as if I was a part of his life and time," she said. His strong handshake impressed her, too. She was just as thrilled and hopeful when she saw him sworn in as president the next morning. She believed that he would stand strongly behind the cause of equal rights and help end segregation. With hindsight, she said in her book, long after he was assassinated, she never changed her mind about President Kennedy.

She felt the time she lived in was more important than her memories of the television shows she appeared on. When she wrote her book, *Movin' on Up*, she gave a great deal of space to her observations of the Kennedys and other politicians and the civil rights movement. Her concern was with Reverend Martin Luther King Jr. and other religious leaders. She tried to sing as much as she could in support of their work and to keep her own singing separate from the hoopla of the entertainment world to which she also very much belonged.

On October 20, 1961, the *Toronto Telegram* would quote her: "Everybody loves God now because he can be sold. But there are still thousands of gospel singers like me, singing just for the joy they get out of it." That year, too, she told writer Alex Haley for an article published in *Reader's Digest*, "Those humble churches are my filling stations. If I didn't get in one every time I can, I would run empty." Many writers heard her say that she had never dreamed her love for church music would earn her so much money. People often pressured her to act "grand" now that she was famous. She didn't want to do that any more than she had wanted to forsake the gospel for the blues when she was young. "I pray that nothing will come between me and God," she told Don Gold, who was writing an article for the *Ladies' Home Journal* in 1963.

9

THE HOLY LAND AT LAST

Not long after President Kennedy's inauguration, Mahalia ended her tours in the United States and set out again for Europe and the Middle East. She had been too ill to continue her European tour in 1952, which she had hoped to finish in Jerusalem. This time when she set sail from New York, as luck would have it, she was sick again. "The one-night stands had sapped my energy and taken my strength. I felt as if somebody had been dragging me across railroad ties," she said in her own book. She worried that history was going to repeat itself. All she did was stay in bed in her stateroom. The stewardess kept bringing her hot tea and soup, but Mahalia couldn't even get up to take a walk on the deck and breathe the fresh air. The ship's doctor told her that her blood pressure was low. She confided in him that she was afraid she wouldn't have the strength to sing in Europe. He promised her that the boat trip would restore her if she would follow his instructions. He ordered her to eat steaks, spinach, and grapes and to drink a glass of wine with every meal. The doctor's advice worked. Finally she got up and watched the water and listened to the sounds of the waves. "The ocean was peaceful and soothing," she said, "and I sat there by myself for hours."

Her audience in England was warm. Though she was still exhausted at times from the rigors of the trip—riding over bad roads in England made her feel as if she were traveling in a wheelbarrow—she knew that she was going to make it this time. Some people from her audiences in Germany told her that she sounded much different in person than she did on records. She explained that she was singing in person with her usual group, without jazzed-up arrangements that had a heavy beat the way they did in the studios. She bought beautiful crystal goblets in Hamburg, Germany, recalling how she had worked for a woman in New Orleans who had been fearful Mahalia would break her crystal. That woman had acted as if the world would have come to an end. Now Mahalia had her own crystal. To add to her personal celebration, she also bought cinnamon rolls and jelly cakes. She felt very fine in Europe.

One Danish reporter asked if she had run into difficulties in the United States because of her color. She told him she had encountered difficulties all her life, but not just because of her race. She wanted to dodge his attempt to make a headline out of a negative comment about her own country.

With so many demands on her time in Europe, she cherished the days when she could go sight-seeing. Among the highlights was her view of the great *Pietà* carved by Michelangelo, which depicts Mary holding her crucified son, Jesus, in her lap. Mahalia had an audience with the pope. Dressed in white robes, he filled her with awe. She felt he was a man of God. And he was especially impressive when he declared that Saint Peter's Basilica was the same as a mother with outstretched arms calling the young to her.

From Rome, Mahalia took a train to Naples, where she boarded a ship to sail across the Mediterranean Sea to the Middle East. She began in Alexandria, Egypt, where the flies and a display of a five-thousand-year-old mummy horrified her. From there she went to Beirut, Lebanon, where the commotion in the streets and the official greetings by

Americans posted abroad offered her none of the spiritual comfort she had expected to find in the Middle East. But her next stop was in Damascus, Syria, where she visited ruins from the Roman Empire. And she began to have a sense of the majestic history of the Old Testament.

She was thrilled to see a church where Saint Paul had preached. Soon she was riding along the old road from Damascus to Jerusalem—"a wild, narrow, dusty road," she said, describing it. Her driver was a "great big Arab man who wore a red fez and right away he and I began to have a time together. Syria has the worst-driving people in the whole world and they must have picked 'Fez' as the prize of the nation." Soon she was hollering at him. He told her "he had never been treated that way before by any woman and he would like to come to the United States and marry me. I told him he had missed his chance. I would never marry a man who drove a car the way he did."

Nevertheless she reached the river Jordan safely, and she got out to bend down and let the water flow over her hands. Its muddy brown color reminded her of the Mississippi River at New Orleans. Soon they passed the Dead Sea, so brilliant an aquamarine color in the sun that it was nearly blinding, and reached the hills of Jericho. She saw Bedouin children with shepherds' crooks herding sheep and goats. The women were veiled and carried jugs on their heads. The tribesmen, who wore turbans, had sheep and camels. Mahalia was certain the scene hadn't changed from the days of the Old Testament. She remembered the spiritual she had often sung about going to talk, shout, and pray high up in Jerusalem one day when she died. And she was almost there.

First she stopped in one of the oldest Christian churches in the world, which a Roman empress, who had become a Christian, had ordered to be built in Bethlehem. "We went slowly down a steep flight of stairs and they left me alone to pray in a candlelit chamber in which there was a rock that is said to mark the spot where stood the manger in which Christ was born," Mahalia said in her book. She was overwhelmed by her surroundings.

93

That afternoon she and Mildred Falls walked in a blooming, sweet-smelling garden tended by silent monks from the old Church of Saint Anne. She saw olive trees that some people believed were two thousand years old. And she walked on the hot, narrow stone streets in Old Jerusalem, which was then governed by Arabs. "I found myself unable to speak as we walked over the same path that our Lord had been driven along by Pontius Pilate's Roman soldiers, bearing His cross." She entered the Church of the Holy Sepulchre and felt that she had been blessed. The visit to Jerusalem felt like a homecoming.

In Israel, where she was planning to sing in Tel Aviv, she was so wrapped up in her own religious fervor and beliefs that she got into a debate with some Israelis when she told them that she was going to bring Christ to the Jews. One of the men had survived the Holocaust in Germany during World War II. She said he was a "good sport about me letting off so much steam. He was the son of a line of seven rabbis, so he wasn't about to change his religion." The concert in Tel Aviv was "fine," she reported. For two hours, "we had a good time—Jews, Arabs, and Christians—all of us together." Then she began to feel the strain of the concert tour and the Holy Land. She dreamed that one day she might go back as a missionary for her church. But she was very happy to be heading home to the United States.

"When we steamed into New York it was just at dawn and the sun came up to blaze on the city's tall buildings and make them look like towers of gold. . . . I was back home again and I felt that when my time came, Heaven would feel like this, too."

10

MAHALIA'S VISION OF FREEDOM

Back in the United States, Mahalia renewed her great interest in the progress of the civil rights movement. Even though the Supreme Court in 1956 had outlawed segregation in bus terminals, the South still required Negroes and whites to use separate waiting rooms, bathrooms, and restaurants. Mahalia watched from afar but with her heart aboard the buses as a militant group of Freedom Riders led by young men from the Congress of Racial Equality boarded a Trailways bus in Washington, D.C., and headed south. In Alabama they were greeted by some die-hard white segregationists. They injured some of the riders.

Reverend King and Reverend Abernathy traveled from Atlanta to Montgomery to hold church services and support the Freedom Riders. In the church, people sang gospel hymns to keep their spirits strong. But the threat of violence was so great that Reverend King went to the basement of the church and called Attorney General Robert F. Kennedy, who then talked with the governor of Alabama. A few minutes later the National Guard arrived at the church and escorted the worshipers safely to their houses.

The Freedom Riders moved on to Mississippi, protected by soldiers and police. They were jailed, but they were making progress. Mahalia was completely devoted to Reverend King and his policy of nonviolent demonstration. After making a gospel-singing tour through the South with Mildred Falls and another friend, Mahalia took her group to Dr. King's house for Thanksgiving dinner with his wife, Coretta, and their children. As Mrs. King was cooking the turkey, friends and relatives arrived—Martin's mother and the family of Reverend Abernathy. Mahalia described a happy gathering around the white tablecloth. Reverend King prayed for peace. The turkey—complemented by collard greens, corn bread, sweet potatoes, and baked ham and followed by pie with ice cream and coffee—made Mahalia feel completely at home. It was an old-fashioned Thanksgiving Day, she said, without any hint of trouble coming. She noticed that whenever the doorbell rang, people arrived to a warm welcome.

Then she left to sing at a revival meeting near Nashville, Tennessee, and to resume her work. Two weeks later she turned on the radio to hear that Reverend King had been arrested and sent to jail for his part in the Albany Movement, a phase of the civil rights movement targeting Albany, Georgia, where people had never been granted their rights, not even the right to vote. Reverend Abernathy, too, was arrested and went to jail. Then he and Dr. King and nine other men working with them were jailed again when they prayed on the steps of City Hall. The churches rallied to support the cause. To Mahalia, who heard that people went to church and sang gospel songs, it was particularly satisfying that the movement found its succor in the churches.

She explained that some of the hymns about people wanting to steal away to Jesus actually meant they wanted to go north, to freedom on earth. She applauded the singing of the song "We Shall Overcome," which had become the anthem of the civil rights movement. Heart and soul, she was involved in the movement, whether she was present at many of its great events or not. She had always been politically involved, attending political conventions and making friends with Democratic politicians, even in the days before she became a well-known singer. She was outspoken in her criticism of any of her own people who were divisive and critical of Reverend Martin Luther King Jr. And she applauded the white and black clergymen who joined the hard and dangerous work of securing equal rights.

In her book, she scolded white Southern Baptist ministers for not speaking out against the people who burned down Negro churches. She was grateful to a group of northern ministers and rabbis who went down to Albany to help. When they were thrown in jail, "the white churches of Albany kept silent," she said. "It beats me how a man can go around preaching about the love of God, whom he has never seen, and scorn his brothers, whom he meets every day on the face of the earth!"

While her mind was occupied with the civil rights activity in the country, she kept traveling "like a mule that has been put back between the shafts," she said in her book. She proved that some progress had been made when she was invited to appear at a reception in Washington, D.C., at the home of Mr. and Mrs. Chester Bowles, who served in the Kennedy administration. Then she performed at Constitution Hall—the same hall that had been closed to the great African-American contralto Marian Anderson in 1939. Mahalia sang several of her favorite gospel songs and "America," too. Afterward, an African-American teenage girl, who had been at the concert, asked her how she could sing "America." With tears in her eyes, the teenager said that the country wasn't free for her own people; it wasn't their country. Mahalia explained, "We're Americans as much as anybody else. What we're going through now means better days ahead for you younger people. I'm one of the last of the old school of Negroes. We had to make it without education. Now you young people have got to get educated. Go back to the school and stay in the church and let men like the Reverend Martin Luther King Jr. show you the way."

She toured in Canada and went as far from home as Japan and Australia in the early 1960s. In 1962 she made her debut at New York's Philharmonic Hall. "For Miss Jackson, it was just another in a series of triumphs. For Philharmonic Hall, it was, one hopes, only the first foray into the complex and vibrant genre of modern gospel music," wrote critic Robert Shelton in the *New York Times* on October 13, 1962. For Mahalia personally, it was another of her many attempts to try to "break down some of the hate and fear that divide the white and colored people in this country," she said. She kept performing at benefit concerts, many for church causes.

On October 1, 1963, she received an honorary doctorate in humane letters from Lincoln College in Illinois. With Governor Otto Kerner at the ceremony, and three hundred people watching, the college president, Dr. Raymond Dooley, told her: "It would be impossible to estimate the number of people who have been gladdened and inspired by your singing." She gave a benefit concert to help raise money for a new three-hundred-thousand-dollar science hall.

The one-night stands on the concert tours wore her out so much that one night, as she was about to sing in St. Louis, she found she couldn't make a sound. She thought she was suffering from exhaustion. Her manager, a man named Lew Mindling, who had begun working for her much earlier, decided to cut short her tour. He insisted she go to a hospital for tests. Mahalia didn't like being there at all, even though it was a luxurious place, "a big white-folks' hospital over on the Chicago Gold Coast where the North Shore millionaires live," she said. She told Mindling she felt like a pincushion, and her voice was getting too high. One night she simply got dressed and walked out of the hospital, saying she would be treated from then on in her own house, and she would sleep in her own bed.

But she was not really well. Doctors had diagnosed her with diabetes and heart trouble; she may have had a heart attack the night that she couldn't sing in St. Louis. For an entire summer she was forced to stay at home and rest. Then she went back to work but limited her schedule to about seventy-five performances a year. "For thirty years, 365 days a year, I'd put on my clothes in a car and hop out to get on stage for one-nighters. I can't anymore," she told Sidney Fields when he interviewed her for his March 31, 1967, column, "Only Human," which had moved to the *New York Daily News.* But she was too involved with the gospel to sit home and retire. Often she had blessed the Lord for giving her the strength to work. All her life, working, especially singing the gospel, had helped her vanquish the loneliness and despair that came from hard times. So she continued the main business of her life: touring to sing the gospel.

One of the great events of her life occurred when she joined the March on Washington in August 1963. She knew that it had been planned first by J. Philip Randolph, a great labor leader for African-American railroad workers, and a shrewd politician who had put pressure on the country to pass the first Fair Employment Practices Bill through Congress. For a while it seemed as if the March on Washington might never take place. Some African-Americans were reluctant to march. They didn't think it would do any good. They were also aware of the violent demonstrations in the South, where people were being beaten up, bombed, and even killed. White people, even those with the best of goodwill, were worried that a March on Washington might erupt into violence. But eventually, African-Americans caught the spirit, mobilized, and decided to demonstrate.

Mahalia was asked to sing at the event, just before Reverend Martin Luther King Jr. delivered a speech at the Lincoln Memorial. On the day of the march, the weather was beautiful and sunny, without the humidity for which Washington was famous. She saw tens of thousands of people "spreading out on the grassy slopes and under the big elms and oaks in the big parks." There were families with small children, and boys and girls playing and racing around, and fathers showing their children the great sights of the Washington Monument and the White House.

She was also impressed and glad to see that everyone was nicely dressed and polite. Police and soldiers seemed to be stationed everywhere, but they had no cause to disturb anybody. Nobody was arrested. Mahalia heard that about two hundred thousand people arrived that day, some on buses and trains, others in planes and cars, and even on foot and on bicycles. Young people who had been working for integration down south came for their first sight of Washington, D.C. Celebrities arrived by the planeload from California. She saw the African-American singer and actress Josephine Baker, who had become a star in Paris, and actor Sidney Poitier, baseball star Jackie Robinson, singer Harry Belafonte, and the great beauty Lena Horne. White actors Marlon Brando, Burt Lancaster, Paul Newman, and Charlton Heston came, along with African-American comedians Sammy Davis, Jr., and Dick Gregory.

Among the prominent figures in the civil rights movement were Mrs. Medgar Evers, widow of the civil rights leader who was killed in cold blood in Alabama; and Daisy Bates, who had led colored children into a white school in Little Rock, Arkansas; classmates of Sunday-school children who had been killed by a bomb in a church in an infamous incident in Birmingham; and Reverend Fred Shuttlesworth, a brave civil rights preacher from Alabama. Everyone wanted to be part of the largest demonstration ever to take place in Washington. And it was peaceful.

Just before noon Mahalia watched people streaming toward the Lincoln Memorial. It was "a parade that you see only once in a lifetime," she said. "Thousands were walking twenty abreast singing hymns and songs, waving American flags and banners and signs about the Civil Rights Bill, flowing like two great rivers toward the memorial. There were old folks in wheelchairs and men and women on crutches. I saw a white man help a colored woman who was marching alone with four children. He picked up one child and they all walked together.

"To me it was like marching with a mighty host that had come for deliverance." At the memorial, she climbed the marble steps toward the great statue of Abraham Lincoln and took her seat. J. Philip Randolph introduced the speakers. All around her were important leaders in the civil rights movement, including Roy C. Wilkins, Martin Luther King Jr., Whitney Young, and John Lewis. White Catholic, Jewish, and Protestant clergymen and white union leaders also attended, as did Dr. Ralph Bunche, who was the U.S. ambassador to the United Nations, and Justice Thurgood Marshall, who had taken the case to desegregate the schools to the Supreme Court and won in 1954.

On that bright sunny day, with the District of Columbia and the Potomac River sparkling, she thought about Marian Anderson, who had sung in that exact same place in 1939, after she was prevented by the Daughters of the American Revolution from singing at Constitution Hall. Supported by Mrs. Eleanor Roosevelt, Miss Anderson had performed at the Lincoln Memorial instead. At the suggestion of Reverend King, Mahalia decided to sing "I Been 'Buked and I Been Scorned," about how she would one day tell the Lord that she had been abused for too long. Everyone joined in with her, clapping and singing. She had pinned her hat on tight, so that she could move around freely and not worry about it falling off; in churches, the combs sometimes flew out of her hair as she moved excitedly with her own music. Studs Terkel would later tell Jules Schwerin about a plane that was flying around, making a loud buzzing noise as Mahalia sang. The noise was not only annoying; it was drowning out Mahalia. She lifted her face and began singing directly at the plane. And her voice drowned out its noise.

Then Dr. King delivered the speech he would become most famous for: "I have a dream that one day on the red hills of Georgia, the sons of former slaves and sons of former slave owners will be able to sit down together at the table of brotherhood. I have a dream that my four little children will one day live in a nation where they will be judged not by the color of their skin but by the content of their character." Mahalia called it the greatest speech of the day. It would soon be recognized as one of the great speeches in the history of the country.

"I may not live to see the complete freedom that Negroes seek come to America, but I got the vision of it that great day," she would say, summing up her impressions of the March on Washington.

About three months later, as she was heading from a hotel to a television show rehearsal in California, Mildred Falls came running up to her and told her that President Kennedy had been shot. Neither woman could believe it. They went to the studio, where they were told that the president was dead. Mahalia went back to the hotel and knelt down on the floor to pray. For her it was a deep personal loss. She considered Kennedy a great friend of African-Americans. Though not everyone agreed with her, Mahalia felt that he had been killed because of racial hatred. She mourned the young president and his "bright light gone from the world," as his widow Jacqueline Kennedy Onassis would soon say eloquently after his assassination in Dallas, Texas.

TURNING POINTS

Mahalia would later say that the person who helped her through her sorrow over the death of President Kennedy was a building contractor named Sigmund Galloway who was building houses for well-to-do African-Americans in California. She had known him, his wife, and his daughter, Sigma, when they lived in Gary, Indiana. Mahalia had often sung there. By 1964, Mrs. Galloway had died, and Sigma was living with Sigmund's mother. Sigmund was reunited with Mahalia in California, where he took her out to dinner and went to all her performances. Forty-seven years old, five years younger than Mahalia, he had *joie de vivre*; he loved to go out and do things in the world. Most of all, he had a knack for cheering up Mahalia when she was tired from work.

Because he had some knowledge of music, they worked out new arrangements for a few of her gospel songs. She asked him to escort her to parties she was invited to attend in Hollywood. By the time she left for a tour of Europe in 1964, she was calling him "Minters," the family's nickname for him.

In Europe, she was so busy that she didn't feel lonesome for him. Like many performers who spend a great deal of their lives on the road, Mahalia always took people along with her on tours—Mildred Falls, other musicians, managers, and additional staff members. Traveling musicians relieved the loneliness and boredom of the road by creating a lifestyle marked by camaraderie. But when the tour ended, Mahalia knew that she would go back to her house at 8353 Indiana Avenue in Chicago, and when she closed the door behind her guests at night, she would feel lonesome. She started giving her relationship with Minters more serious thought. If he wanted to continue seeing her, she thought he had better watch out. And so should she, she reminded herself. She had been married and divorced once already, and no other man she had met had turned out to be a good match for her.

Galloway wanted to keep seeing her. The tall, handsome, dignified-looking man even wanted to marry her. Not everybody liked him as much as she did. Although she found him attractive, and she was in love with him, she was far from a naive young woman. Laurraine Goreau reported in her book that Mahalia and Galloway even signed a prenuptial agreement based on Mahalia's earnings, to protect her in the event that the marriage didn't work out. One of her close business associates didn't like Galloway and told her not to expect him to be able to work with the man. Fans who saw pictures of the couple even wrote to Mahalia, advising her not to marry Galloway, because they thought he was white; he was a very light-skinned man. Mahalia answered them that he simply looked white standing next to her because she was quite dark. She dismissed those sorts of letters and decided to go ahead with the marriage.

At the same time, Mahalia and Mildred Falls came to a parting of the ways. People were puzzled that the women, who had enjoyed such a close friendship for twenty years, would suddenly end it. They had loved their work together; Mildred had known exactly when Mahalia was going to breathe. Musically they were a perfect pair. Offstage, both big women loved good, fattening, southern-style cooking. Exactly what caused the breakup wasn't made clear. One version of the story suggests that their friendship ended because of Galloway. Mahalia later suggested that Galloway wanted to take charge of her career. Since Mildred and Mahalia were such close collaborators, Galloway may have wanted to get Mildred out of his way. He may have found a way to come between the women. But Jules Schwerin heard from Little Brother John Sellers that Mahalia simply fired Mildred, because she asked for a raise of one hundred dollars.

Mahalia had hired Mildred for two hundred dollars a week plus hotel expenses on the road. When Mahalia began earning great sums of money, she kept paying Mildred the same salary. John Sellers had squabbles about money with Mahalia himself. He thought she became increasingly stingy and "grand," he said, as she became rich. He heard her try to settle arguments by telling people she was Mahalia Jackson and not to argue with that fact. Actually her strong will was nothing new. She had always known the power of her own talent and presence. And she had always pinched pennies. She couldn't break that habit even when she no longer had to hoard every coin anymore.

John Sellers took a musical direction that Mahalia didn't approve of. He became a jazz and blues artist, working closely with blues star Big Bill Broonzy and making records for the pop music market. Sellers and Mahalia lost some of their good feeling for each other as time passed. As an adult he was in and out of her life. Whether Mildred fought with Mahalia over money or Galloway or something else, when Galloway came into Mahalia's life, Mildred went out.

At her wedding, the only people at the ceremony in her living room were Polly Fletcher, Mahalia's secretary and longtime friend, Lew Mindling, her manager, and the pastor of the Greater Salem Baptist Church. Mahalia wore her best blue dress and a corsage. She had been alone since her divorce from Ike Hockenhull. Such a long time, she thought. She wanted to celebrate the end of her lonesomeness.

Sigmund's daughter, Sigma, came to stay with the couple. Mahalia pretended to be so happy that she dedicated her book, *Movin' on Up*, to Sigmund and Sigma, calling them her husband and daughter. But the marriage was actually a strain for her. Two months after the ceremony, she was hospitalized with a heart attack at the Little Company of Mary Hospital in Chicago. President Lyndon Johnson, who had succeeded to the White House after President Kennedy's assassination, sent her a letter, after she had to cancel an official performance for him. She received so many flowers that she joked she thought she had died.

But she was sick and couldn't work or enjoy life. Both she and Minters were miserable. For the next two years she was in and out of hospitals a dozen times. By April 1966, the marriage was over, and the next year Mahalia discussed her marriage failures in an article in *Ebony* magazine.

She said that her first husband had been a weak man who had loved her as she was, and the second husband had been a strong man who loved her for what she was and what she could do for him. In other words, both men had tried to use her in their own ways, she felt. But she had thought she knew Galloway well enough to make the decision to marry and build a happy life with him.

It turned out that Minters still wanted to go out and have a good time. But Mahalia didn't have the strength or desire. She had always worked very hard and traveled by car to save money. Then she wanted to go home, cook for friends, and live a quiet life. When she went out, she didn't want to go to places that weren't proper for a churchwoman. Minters always wanted to go bowling, play golf, or go to the theater—things she didn't do. She had known about his tastes before she married him, and they had worried her a bit. But both of them were Baptists from church-oriented families. She had hoped they could work out their differences. Then she discovered there was no way to predict what would happen to a couple after the marriage ceremony.

She found out that Minters wanted her to advance his musical career, and he made fun of her gospel songs, unable to understand how she drew such great crowds for that type of music. He went into a kind of competition with her. She got her record company to make a recording of him playing the flute. But still he didn't achieve the fame she had painstakingly earned for her own genius over the years.

She knew she had made a mistake by marrying a young, ambitious man. Jules Schwerin wrote that Minters liked to drink Scotch and go out with other women. Mahalia nagged him, Minters said. She didn't want to let people know she had made a fool of herself. So she kept trying to make the marriage work. When he corrected the way she talked, even when she was being interviewed by the press, she let his criticisms go by without fighting. He wanted to boss her around. She wanted a quiet companion when the applause stopped.

Each time she was hospitalized during her marriage, the doctors found nothing wrong with her, she said. She even saw a psychiatrist, who told her she was as sound as a dollar, she claimed. But her friends no longer came to join her for meals, as they had once felt free to do. Some people actually told her that her husband was slick and no good. Schwerin wrote that Mahalia didn't like the mean way Minters looked at her. Finally, after one disagreement too many, the couple separated. Mahalia left him in her house. Then she had to fight to get him out of there.

During the divorce trial, she went down to 160 pounds and worried that she was going to end up looking like a skeleton. She was a woman who had cured herself of rickets by eating as well as she could in New Orleans. Food had always symbolized a cure and a joy for her. The doctors were pleased with her weight loss because it eased the strain on her heart. But she was unaccustomed to weighing under 200 pounds. She felt that she had lost her health during the marriage.

Actually she had worked hard all her life. Each time she sang, she did so with all the energy in her body. A few people in her audiences sometimes worried that she would wear out her lungs. But she thought her second marriage had been the worst strain. And she rued her marital failures.

A poor woman who had love had everything, she philoso-phized, and love was the most important thing in a woman's life. With love, she felt, a person could stand up and fight the world. A career had its limitations, she believed. No matter how great a career was, it could end and leave a life empty. It could never take the place of love. She knew that her first husband had actually loved her, despite his weakness for gambling. He had never remarried because he would never love anyone but her, he said. But she couldn't adjust to his craziness with money. Now she wondered if she could have helped him somehow.

Despite the wreckage of her marriages, she counted her blessings. She believed that the love of God was always with her. She had her career, and she was trying to help talented young people through the Mahalia Jackson Foundation. With the funds she had been raising for the foundation since the early 1960s, she hoped to construct a nondenominational temple of worship one day. Even the Rockefeller family may have contributed to her project. In 1961 she had founded an annual scholarship for a music student—"a deserving person, whether Negro or white," she had specified—at Roosevelt University in Chicago. She insisted that she wanted to help youngsters get an education. She hoped to discover a young woman as talented as Pearl Bailey, who had sung gospel music, then grown up to be a jazz singer, an entertainer, and eventually a friend and adviser of United States presidents. Pearl Bailey had even served as a U.S. ambassador to the United Nations. Mahalia wanted to find another Marian Anderson someplace, too, who could be helped through her foundation and find love and purpose in the world.

Mahalia's voice faltered in this period. She sounded weak for a while. But as time passed, she recovered her strength and power. She began working again. Her health would have its ups and downs from then on, however. In the spring of 1967, she sang in excellent form on Easter Sunday at Philharmonic Hall in New York. Then, in late summer, she undertook another tour of Europe. In Germany, her first stop, she was asked by a thrilled audience to do an encore on a television show. She was supposed to go on from West Germany to Britain, Switzerland, and Italy. But the day after the television show, she collapsed and was taken to Westend Hospital in West Berlin; the diagnosis was exhaustion. She stayed there for about a week until doctors let her go home. The tour was canceled. After a little rest in Chicago, she managed to go on singing.

The next year, however, she was shocked and her faith severely tested—perhaps more than it had ever been. The Reverend Martin Luther King Jr. was shot and killed on the balcony of a motel where he was staying in Memphis, Tennessee, on April 4, 1968. Mahalia went to Atlanta to take part in the funeral. She was interviewed by Judith Martin for a *Washington Post* story on April 9, 1968. Mahalia's voice was shaking.

"I'm oppressed. I'm burdened and I'm hurt," Mahalia said. "Since the shock of his death, I have tried to think reasonably that this is God's will. But the pressures weaken its effectiveness. Thus, I've faltered."

Miss Martin knew that Mahalia had heart trouble. In a quiet room at the Regency Hotel, she lay on her bed, wearing blue nylon pajamas under a blue nylon robe.

"With a little rest," she said, "I'll be sharp." She was going to sing Dr. King's favorite song, "Precious Lord," at his funeral that day.

She had been performing at benefits to raise money for Dr. King's work and had last seen him on New Year's Eve in Chicago. At a holiday party, they had sung a spiritual together: "Jesus, Lover of My Soul." He had told her, "This type of song is what holds me up in my hours of prayer."

Mahalia said she was afraid of the dangers coming from all sides in the streets. "Who wants to live in a furnace of hell?" she asked. "When I was very, very poor I had more peace of mind because I didn't know all the evils of people wanting things and letting something stand in their way." She heaved a big sigh. "And yet I am contented with my life now because it is what God wills."

This was the woman who had once said she asked nothing more than to be able to sing the gospel for the rest of her life. Even at this time she was trying not to question the Lord or her faith in Him. But the struggle was enormous. She had always known there were reasons for discontent—with show business, with parasites on the gospel highway, and with racist fools. But the good news had always been victorious and convinced her to keep trying. Now her hopes, which centered on the young leader, had been dashed.

The police tracked down the killer, James Earl Ray, a native of Tennessee, who went to trial in Memphis and was sentenced to life imprisonment.

On June 5, two months later, Robert Kennedy, whom Mahalia had admired so much, was assassinated in Los Angeles. Once again she was felled by grief. She appeared on CBS television to sing "I Been 'Buked and I Been Scorned" a cappella in his honor. Tears streamed down her cheeks. Whatever her personal problems, she had seen herself clearly as a part of the momentous political changes in the country in the 1960s. She had spent precious time and energy putting the gospel at the service of the best instincts of the people who were devoting their lives to progress. Now she was watching some of the country's best young men being killed off senselessly. Her vision of a bright future had been blurred by her own tears.

12

GOING HOME

In the next year, Mahalia spoke often about Reverend Martin Luther King Jr. saying that she never thought of him as an ordinary man. "God had to send that man to wake up his people," she told writer Granville Watts in an interview. "And many called him Moses. Whatever name they called him, he was sent from God."

Benjamin Hooks, a civil rights lawyer and businessman who headed the NAACP in the 1970s, came to know Mahalia well. He understood the prejudice she had met as a woman and as an African-American, and he admired the intelligence and shrewdness with which she handled her career and business affairs in the church and in the secular world. He knew she always insisted on being paid in cash for her performances because of all the times she had been cheated as a younger woman. If, during her twenty years as a star, she never forgot the difficulties of her first forty years, that was to be expected, he thought. He told Jules Schwerin that Dr. King's influence on the destiny of African-Americans and his untimely violent death had an enormous impact on Mahalia: "The ground he walked on, to her, was holy." Mahalia and Dr. King had special respect for each other's gifts and goals.

After he died, she kept singing and traveling, putting all the fire she could muster up into her performances. She didn't sound as energetic all the time as she had in earlier years, but she made up for her weariness by using the mastery of her art she had acquired through years of experience. She remained the most majestic, best-known gospel singer in the world to most people. Valerie Wilmer, a well-known writer about jazz, heard a concert by Mahalia late in her life and wrote about it for *Down Beat* magazine:

> *Miss Jackson's recent heart attacks have obviously left her a little weak, and she was [in] a subdued mood for most of the concert [at Royal Albert Hall in London]. Accordingly, she paced herself carefully. . . . Miss Jackson's simple reading of "My Living" was one of the concert's memorable moments along with a compelling "How Great Thou Art," but there was an underlying air of melancholy in her approach to telling the Gospel story. It is always sad to see an artist who has been felled by illness, yet Miss Jackson is well on the way to coping. Just when you think that she is slipping from the magniloquent to the mundane, she'll hit one of those indescribable, pene-trating notes that pins you back in your seat. . . . Mahalia has, regrettably, lost something of that in-explicable magnificence that made hers the most majestic and unsurpassable voice in the world, and yet she keeps coming back. On one funky, slow song which had a bluesy piano accompaniment nearer to the secular than the sacred, she sang the words "I had a friend" with such poignance that "friend" went right through me in a way that recalled the harsh defiance of the queen of secular song, Bessie Smith.*
>
> *It's at moments like these that the simplicity, the reality of both Gospel music and the mighty Mahalia herself is realized . . . [And] living indeed seemed not in vain.*

Mahalia could still communicate that inspired idea to audiences.

About her private, life, Little Brother John Sellers struck some minor notes, Jules Schwerin wrote. By 1967, Mahalia had bought and combined two condominiums high up in a building on Chicago's South Side, and she moved there, leaving behind her ranch-style house and her memories of a failed marriage. John Sellers needed a job. His musical career was not supporting him at that time. He went to work as valet, chef, and household manager in Mahalia's aerie for five hundred dollars a week. He moved in, too.

He watched her fire an African-American law firm that had handled her affairs, collecting high fees, for many years. In its place she hired a young white lawyer who had been recommended to her by a new friend, the wife of a prominent African-American architect. Sellers had no idea what might have made Mahalia dissatisfied with the services of her former firm.

John Sellers also kept in touch with Mildred Falls. Though he had renewed relations with Mahalia after a very bad fight, Mahalia and Mildred never became friends again to his knowledge. Mildred was ill and in great need of money, but she didn't ask Mahalia for any help, Sellers believed.

Mahalia's lawyer and various other staff people in charge of her business affairs reported to work every day in her apartment, where she had set up an office for them. John Sellers was under the impression that Mahalia loved having her staff in the house. She charged higher fees than ever before for her singing engagements. At times he actually told Mahalia about how "grand" and mighty he thought she had become, living so high up in a building. From her vantage point, she had many disappointments to rise above. But the tensions between them didn't last, Sellers said. They sometimes spent evenings together reminiscing about the tough but good old days when he was a little boy sleeping in a bed between Mahalia and Ike.

Though she knew her health could take a turn for the worse at any time, Mahalia didn't shrink from scheduling foreign tours. In the spring of 1971, she performed a ninety-minute concert in New Delhi, India. At the end, the audience asked her to keep singing. She stayed onstage for three hours before one thousand people, including the U.S. ambassador to India, Kenneth B. Keating, and Prime Minister Indira Gandhi, who postponed meetings with top-level government officials to stay and hear every note. Mahalia sang the anthem of the civil rights movement, "We Shall Overcome," for Mrs. Gandhi, to her particular delight.

Her gospel songs and the management of her affairs constituted her daily activities. She even invested in a fast-food chicken business. Benjamin Hooks, who took part in the negotiations to include her, respected her clear mind and business acumen. She may have missed out on high school mathematics courses, but she more than made up for the lack with what she had taught herself over the years. She never married again, though she stayed in touch with both of her ex-husbands, talking by phone to Galloway but appearing to prefer her friendship with Ike Hockenhull. He had never intentionally tried to harm her in any way.

In 1972, she had to go to the hospital again for a variety of complaints. Her heart was unable to withstand the strain of the illnesses and treatments that might have helped her. So it was no great surprise when the news came out, first in a brief Associated Press story on January 27, 1972, and then in newspapers, magazines, and broadcasts: Mahalia Jackson, at age sixty, had died of a heart seizure that day in the Little Company of Mary Hospital in Chicago.

According to Jules Schwerin, her estate may have been worth as much as nine million dollars, including all of her real estate holdings, royalties, and investments. In her will, she may have left two thousand dollars to Mildred Falls, but Mildred probably never received it. Exactly why was not explained, but an estate that large can take a long time to be settled, and Mildred Falls died about two years after Mahalia. John Sellers received nothing in the will, according to Schwerin's book.

Sellers was supposed to sing at Mahalia's funeral, but at the last moment, to his great dismay, he was taken off the

114

schedule. Instead, Aretha Franklin arrived in Chicago to sing a moving, emotional version of "Precious Lord." Mahalia herself would have applauded it. Her body lay in state in the Greater Salem Baptist Church and then was moved, by order of Mayor Daley, to the Arie Crown Theater at McCormick Place, just off Lake Shore Drive, for a memorial service. It was attended by a crowd of ten thousand mourners, including Martin Luther King's widow, Coretta Scott King. "Death is a mean man!" the Reverend Joseph H. Jackson said in his eulogy, evoking a time-honored theme from the world of the African-American Baptist gospel singing. "I pray that fellow mourners and the grass and the breezes be gentle with my friend." Aretha's father, the eloquent Reverend Clarence L. Franklin, said, "Mahalia lived in a house she tried to repair. And now Mahalia has moved on, on to her other house." Some people sighed; others shouted "Amen."

Ike Hockenhull came to the funeral in a wheelchair. Sigmund Galloway came, too. In her book, Laurraine Goreau said that Galloway had wanted to visit Mahalia in the hospital during her last illness, but was regarded as an annoyance and wasn't allowed to see her. At that time, he didn't know he was sick himself. He would die from cancer four months after Mahalia. Ike Hockenhull also died before the end of a year. Oddly enough, Mahalia's aunt Hannah, whose illnesses had deprived Mahalia of the chance to go to nursing school—a chance that might have led her to forfeit a gospel career—outlived Mahalia.

From Chicago, Mahalia's body was flown to New Orleans for a burial service attended by thousands of mourners, including some survivors in her family. Her brother, Peter, had died about fifteen years earlier. Aunt Duke, with whom she had maintained a good relationship after she established a life in Chicago, had also died, and Mahalia's father was gone. The funeral procession had a motorcycle police escort, a color guard of three marines and a man from each of the armed services, and Baptist ministers. President Richard M. Nixon, for whom she had also performed, sent a message about Mahalia's gift to mankind. Civil rights leaders and prominent entertainers delivered eulogies and praises. Singer Harry Belafonte said of her: "She was the single most powerful black woman in the United States, the woman-power for the grass roots. There was not a single field-hand, a single black worker, a single black intellectual who did not respond to her civil rights message."

She was buried in Providence Memorial Park in Metairie, a New Orleans suburb. Though Mahalia had never seen a typical New Orleans funeral service for a woman in her lifetime, marching bands played dirges for her. After she was buried, the bands turned around and struck up their joyful, swinging, spiritual music on the way back home. People danced in the road, performing the traditional, happy Second-Line celebration. Mahalia had known that people in New Orleans cried at the incoming, the birth of a child, and rejoiced at the outgoing, the death and passage into eternal life. She was now part of that heritage.

She had often sung about how "The Lord Is Going to Separate the Wheat from the Tares"—the wheat from the chaff. That was within the power of the Lord to do, she knew. It was far more difficult for her to know exactly what decisions to make about her personal relationships for her ultimate happiness. Her gospel singing and her goals required so much watchfulness, energy, time, and sacrifice that her personal life was never as happy as her onstage life. Some people said she had learned not to trust anyone. But there had been people in her life for many years whom she had befriended and trusted—Studs Terkel, for one. She idolized Reverend King. In her busy, full life, she had revered, nurtured, and loved others, too.

So much had happened to her, and she had caused so much to happen. Gospel music had rescued her during a childhood filled with loneliness and desperation. Perhaps it had eventually isolated her, when her singing made her such a superstar and an inspiration to others that she couldn't live an ordinary existence. But she had achieved her goal of helping to bridge the gap between the races. That was one of the most important jobs facing all Americans. "The granddaughter of a slave, she had struggled for years for fulfillment and for unprejudiced recognition of her talent," wrote Alden Whitman in her obituary in the *New York Times*.

During the twenty-five years after her death, many memorial concerts have been staged as tributes to her. Enterprising theater people have attempted to produce her life story on the Broadway and off-Broadway stage. It's ironic that Mahalia herself would not have gone to see those shows. None really did her justice. Into the 1990s she still merited stories in the country's leading newspapers and magazines. Columbia and Apollo reissued her songs on compact discs. And the flame of her singing was reignited every time a recording was played. Though she had hoped to find talented youngsters to replace her, so far no one had been able to do so.

BIBLIOGRAPHY

Goreau, Laurraine. *Just Mahalia, Baby.* Gretna, La.: Pelican Publishing Company, 1975.

Harris, Michael W. *The Rise of Gospel Blues: The Music of Thomas Andrew Dorsey in the Urban Church.* New York: Oxford University Press, 1992.

Heilbut, Anthony. *The Gospel Sound: Good News and Bad Times.* New York: Limelight Editions, 1992.

Jackson, Mahalia, with Evan McLeod Wylie. *Movin' on Up.* New York: Hawthorn Books, 1966.

Stearns, Marshall W. *The Story of Jazz.* New York: Oxford University Press, 1958.

Newspapers and periodicals referred to for background material are the *New York Times*, New York *Daily News*, *Newsweek*, *Time*, *Ebony*, *The Reporter*, the *New York World-Telegram and Sun*, the *Washington Post*, *New York Post*, *Harper's* magazine, *Reader's Digest*, the *New York Daily Mirror*, the *Saturday Evening Post*, *Rhythm and Blues* magazine, the *Melody Maker*, the Associated Press news service, a transcript from the television show *Night Beat* hosted by Mike Wallace, and a CBS promo for *Mahalia*, her network radio show, which made its debut in October 1954.

SELECTED DISCOGRAPHY

Mahalia Jackson: The Apollo Sessions, 1946–1951.
  Pair Records, courtesy of Apollo Records/Bess Music,
  1994.

This album contains some of her fifty earliest records,
  including her first best–seller, "I Will Move on up a
  Little Higher."

Mahalia Jackson, Live at Newport, 1958, Columbia
  Legacy, 1994. This is the sound-track album of her
  great concert at the jazz festival in Rhode Island.

Jazz on a Summer's Day, videotape. Raven Films 1959,
  1987.
  Portions of the Newport Concert were captured on
  this video.

INDEX

124

ABOUT THE AUTHOR

Leslie Gourse has researched and written for various mediums including CBS and the *New York Times*. Since 1974, Ms. Gourse has been a freelance writer. Her articles and stories have appeared in numerous magazines and newspapers, covering general culture, social trends, and music. Ms. Gourse won an ASCAP award in 1991 for a series of articles on women that led to her book, *Madam Jazz.*